Praise for *Findings from the Hunting Party's Scout—*

A Rainbow Book

"Delightful, breezy, enchanting to read! Karyn, in this her first book, details one woman's midlife search to find spirit and meaning in life. A successful professional with a devoted husband, two great kids, and a lovely home, nevertheless, she knows that life can offer her more. Her corporate job is not satisfying yet affords her a lifestyle she is not quite ready to give up.

"Karyn's journey from 'soccer mom' and financial consultant to author and worship service leader, evolves because she knows she is a messenger of a deeper truth or reality. Her story will reach many men and women who also feel this ache of separation and hunger for spirituality. Like Elizabeth Gilbert in the very successful *Eat, Pray, Love,* Karyn brings us on a wonderful rich journey of shamans, meditation teachers, writing and career coaches, psychotherapists, mystery school teachers and to places as diverse as pyramids in Egypt, castles in Southern France, Stonehenge in England, and to Tennessee, California and New York. Her search leads her to find peace in her own backyard and the life she has created. So many will be enchanted and inspired by her journey.

"I can't wait to hear more about the next stages of Karyn's journey."

—Allie Roth, Career and Life Coach,
Director, Center for Creativity and Work

"As I read Karyn's book, I was immediately drawn into her faith-filled journey. By the time I had finished reading, I realized that her story was a catalyst for the revitalization of my own journey."

—The Reverend Hope Johnson, Minister, Unitarian Universalist
Congregation of Central Nassau, Garden City, NY

"Author Karyn O'Beirne captures the real essence of a woman's transformational journey through a collection of remarkable stories of courage, love, gratitude and acceptance. *Findings from the Hunting Party's Scout* will spur you inward for fresh discovery. A journey guaranteed to awaken the Soul, unleash your creative power and enlighten your aliveness."

—Marsh Engle, Creative Life Consultant, Author & Founder of
Amazing Woman's Day (www.MarshEngle.com)

"With humor, commitment to naked truth, and richly detailed stories both ordinary and extraordinary, Karyn O'Beirne chronicles her personal evolution in consciousness as again and again she slips between the veil that seems to separate the human self from the Divine Self, each time bringing back more of the Divine to infuse the human experience. We are the Hunting Party, and Karyn is a wise and delightful Scout."

—Gloria Jean, co-author of *The Marriage of Sex & Spirit,
Relationships at the Heart of Conscious Evolution*

More Praise for *Findings from
the Hunting Party's Scout*—

"Karyn O'Beirne's *Finding from the Hunting Party's Scout* takes the reader on a journey where we witness her innermost searching and questions. We also observe the many unique ways she receives an answer from her intuition, higher Self, the unknown, or God. The book's journey is comparable to traveling with a close friend with access to their diary and their innermost thoughts.

"Karyn opens her Self literally to examination bringing herself and the reader into awareness of the depth of her emotions and spiritual yearnings. Karyn's words help the reader to understand the transition and incorporation of a spiritual life into the everyday mundane. Her words serve as a guiding light to remind the reader to live deliberately, appreciate your loved ones for whom they are, and your circumstances as they are. Her words create a desire in the reader to find their own Truth, that we are the creators of our own lives, and to be receptive and open to the Divine in each of us.

"This journey leads us to the discovery that the search never ends 'just keep hunting', whether we are visiting foreign lands or right in our own back yard. Karyn's findings are uniquely her own, yet universally a part of each of us. Go along for the journey, it's worth the trip, and you never know, you may find a little of your-Self along the way."

—Amy Okrepkie, Owner, Healing Touch Wellness Center, LLC

"Karyn invites us on a spiritual journey and vision quest—a captivating personal challenge that lifts us off the story-teller's page into a modern hero's inner life of global adventure and self discovery. Departing on a passage of fate, she leaves her worried-working, soccer-mom-life to become a seeker of integrity, asking, 'What is life really for?'

"With the support of family, faith and friends, she takes up the spiritual artist's task. She paints colorful portraits of transformational workshops, painful self study, remarkable meditations, lucid dreaming, and sacred journeys to holy sites most people only yearn for.

""Globe-trotting Karyn discovers in the journey that her home life holds the answers to her desperate questions. She reveals her intimate struggle with the mother who left her — and recovers a cherished respect for family lost and family found. She ultimately learns to consciously choose trust over self hatred and despair.

"Karyn battles our collective human compulsions and distractions — our old-dream habits of playing small, while blaming and complaining away our responsibility to stretch ourselves and grow. She resists falling backward into self-limiting darkness.

"Karyn captures lightning in a bottle — arriving at spiritual maturity as a Dream Warrior. Her weapons of choice are words to spread the light of human concern — showering kindness and non-judgment on life's ordinary lessons. Her epic voyage ends in her initiation as a writer and minister."

—Ken Nelson, Ph.D., trainer of transformational
workshop leaders worldwide (www.PowerfulWorkshops.com)

Findings from the Hunting Party's Scout

Karyn O'Beirne

Rainbow Books, Inc.
FLORIDA

Library of Congress Cataloging-in-Publication Data

O'Beirne, Karyn, 1958-
  Findings from the hunting party's scout / Karyn O'Beirne. — 1st ed.
    p. cm.
  Includes bibliographical references (p.).
  ISBN 1-56825-113-0 (softcover : alk. paper)
  1. O'Beirne, Karyn, 1958- 2. Unitarian Universalists—New York—Biography.
  I. Title.
  BX9869.O24A3 2008
  289.1092—dc22
  [B]

2008011499

Findings from the Hunting Party's Scout
Copyright © 2008 Karyn O'Beirne
ISBN-13: 978-1-56825-113-4
ISBN-10: 1-56825-113-0

Author's Website: www.Karyn.info

Published by
Rainbow Books, Inc.
P. O. Box 430
Highland City, FL 33846-0430
www.RainbowBooksInc.com

Editorial Offices and Wholesale/Distributor Orders
Telephone (863) 648-4420
Email: RBIbooks@aol.com
www.RainbowBooksInc.com

Individuals' Orders
Toll-free Telephone (800) 431-1579
www.BookCH.com

First edition 2008

12 11 10 09 08   5 4 3 2 1
Printed in the United States of America.

To
Beth,
Good luck and
lots of inspiration —
in your new
adventure —
we are lucky to
have you in the
faith.

Lots
of love, Kay orz

For
Andrew & Garrett

Contents

Preface   ix

Prelude   xi

If here you have found freedom   1

The world stands out on either side   11

To live deliberately   12

Faith of the larger Liberty   19

Find a stillness   23

Kum ba yah   33

Lighting the Chalice   43

Gathered here in the mystery   65

Here on the paths to everyday   81

Enter, rejoice and come in   90

Do not be conformed to this world   96

I am being driven into an unknown land   102

Every morning the world is created   108

Beauty is before me   119

Now I recall my childhood   126

Existence is beyond the power of words to define   131

Named unnamed   143

This is the truth that passes understanding   148
With joy we claim the growing light   157
Since what we choose is what we are   163
In the struggles we choose for ourselves   170
We are here to abet creation and to witness it   179
The limits of tyrants   183
A new manifestation is at hand   185
We receive fragments of holiness, glimpses of eternity   194

Acknowledgements   197
Connections   198
Bibliography   199
Endquotes   201
About the Author   203

Preface

Findings from the Hunting Party's Scout offers up an original perspective on mystical awakening. Breezy in tone, discerning and fast paced, the story is of a modern, married-with-children, working woman looking for a life with more mystery and tenderness. Left searching in an often graceless society racing and immersed in a daily routine of ever longer to do lists, my true story begins when I stumble upon a path presented by a mystic from a long line of shamans.

Propelled forward by the events of September 11 and the memory of New York City becoming empty of life from my office window, I followed my heart to medieval castles in southern France and a pilgrimage to the pyramids in Teotihuacan, Mexico. Teachers were sought, found and some were left along the way. While visiting Ireland's Holy Mountain my deepest questions are answered with unequivocal answers.

But the story does not end on a remote mountain top. The journey continues when I open myself up to the rich opportunities in my own backyard. The awakening takes root in places visited daily; the train station, the ball field, the candle-lit living room. As I came to embrace a spiritual existence with the same assurance that I lived my physical life I felt an undeniable need to write, and ultimately share, what I had found.

Discover real-life spiritual adventure revealed by someone who not so long ago was where you are now – uneasy, cynical and curious. There is nothing to do, no steps to take but your own. Start by realizing the journey isn't for someone else, someone different. The journey is for you.

Prelude

I find myself with thirty people sitting in a circle in an odd assortment of mismatched dining room chairs. We have assembled for a retreat in the woods in central New Jersey, far away from our usual suburban weekend chores. Our feet are firmly planted on the ground below us. I look straight ahead and keep my chin parallel to the ground while resting my palms lightly on my thighs. This is known as the Dreaming position. I hear a woman's soft voice from the middle of the circle tell us to close our eyes.

"Imagine you and Miguel are walking along the beach," she says. "Feel the sand between your toes. Feel the ocean breeze, smell the scent of salt in the air. Look down, see your feet; start to run." I haven't seen Don Miguel for some time, but his face is easy to conjure up. There is nothing distinctive about his face or physical appearance. His wisdom and loving countenance are what make him remarkable as a spiritual teacher and a man.

At first I find it difficult to sustain the images of water, sky, Miguel and the sand together in my mind. But after a few minutes, the scene becomes more real and creating action within the dream gets easier. The ocean does not disappear when I focus on the sand. The sky stays blue without the forced thought of color. The room and my fellow seekers fade as the interior of my mind creates a vista as real as any that ever graced a beach-worthy day.

Soon bored with running on the sand, I start leaping forward with great strides. As the leaps get higher, I become more daring and decide to do a mid-air somersault. This is a dream, I remember, why not! The action is effortless, as gravity is nearly non-existent in my newly created adventure. I flip gracefully in a series of back flips, confidently hitting the sand with hands and feet like an Olympic gymnast. My spirit is elated as my body is supple.

Tumbling and twirling without the boundaries of reality reminds me of a scene in the movie *Crouching Tiger, Hidden Dragon*. I begin to make ninja-like moves while leaping into the air. I hang suspended for a moment before I drop down and leap again. Crouching Mom, Hidden Warrior.

This-Is-Incredible. I open my arms and spread my human wings. Throwing caution to the wind, I leap skyward, air borne; I ride the air currents like a sea gull. Not quite satisfied, I fly into the wind so I am lifted up and somersault powerfully above the sand dunes. I notice that Miguel has joined me, and we begin swooping up, down, and around — kites on a windy day — but we are not tethered by any line. Our actions are controlled by my mind, and I am aware of this.

After several longer flights into the wind, soaring with every gust, I hear Miguel utter his first words, "Do you want to go higher?" he asks. I pause and admit that I am afraid. Without conscious thought, I am quickly pulled up into the stratosphere looking down upon my abundant blue-green home. The earth is beautiful, round and vulnerable.

Unbelievably, I am not afraid to be in space: weightless, airless and without protection. The perspective is so different, so unexpected, I float, experiencing how astounding space is. How delicious to be here with the stars, I muse, thinking unfamiliar thoughts; to be among them, to be of the same stuff as them, and perhaps, even to be one of them. I feel my beloved teacher close by, and while drifting among the stars and gazing down upon the earth, I relay this thought to him:

"So, this is what it is like to be God."

If here
you have
found
freedom

JOE AND I HAVE NO EXPECTATIONS FOR OUR WEEK AT OMEGA. WE HAVE NO expectations because we have no idea what to expect. We have never done anything remotely like this before. The last time I visited Rhinebeck was for the Dutchess County Fair. The view of the Hudson River Valley from our speeding mini-van is as beautiful as I remember, but after sundown we slow down to avoid ending up in a ditch beside the dark country road.

The brochure with our confirmation said it was very important to go to the orientation the night before the weeklong workshop begins. I use my cell phone and leave a message on their general voice mailbox, letting them know we will be late but are definitely coming. We laugh about the call after we hear the orientation. Our fears of not belonging dissipate within the first hour, thanks to the amateur comedian who gives the de-stressing, irreverent orientation. The middle-aged announcer pokes fun at people's sense of spiritual superiority. He holds up that idea and reveals it for what it is — baloney. Spirituality is not a competition or a badge to wear. Relax, he tells us, and don't take yourself or anything else too seriously.

Whew, what a relief, we suspected we were going to be out of our league here. We've been anxious that we might be seen as impostors, not sufficiently enlightened to be here at all. We learn at orientation that this week at Omega is known as Retreat Week. Now we have a label for where we are when we are asked where we have been when we get back home. We have no words to explain to anybody what we are doing. Spiritual yearnings are an unspoken topic with our family, friends and co-workers. Now we can say we were on a retreat and hope to leave the explanation of our absence at that.

After a good laugh, a cup of tea, and ice cream, we make our way to our cabin. Joe insisted on coming to the retreat with me and requested I reserve a cabin with our own bathroom, the most expensive option. I, in turn, requested abstinence for the five days we will be here.

Usually, being married with children, any time away alone, together, is an exercise in having the best possible, uninterrupted sex. All activities are perceived as foreplay when we are without the kids. I adamantly refuse to engage in all that sexual maneuvering. I let Joe come with me, but I am not the entertainment. I am here to learn something. I am here for me. Luckily there are two double beds, and Joe wisely decides we will each have our own for the week.

My husband's narrow frame of reference and basic intolerance of unusual people worries me. We will probably see some odd looking people here this week. Further, the food is mostly vegetarian. There is no liquor or bars around for miles. I do not want my experience to be colored by his potentially acidic response to the retreat. I do not want to return his sarcastic remarks with defensive explanations about my decision to come to the workshop in the first place. I am already worried about overcoming my own cynicism. What am I doing here anyway? What am I looking for? Happiness is the answer. What is unfamiliar is to be taking the time and spending the money to look for happiness here.

Our first full day, we soak up the place. We breathe it in while walking the paths to the dining hall and to class. We eat the holistic essence with every meal we share with our fellow guests. The campus exists as a euphoric bubble inside the larger, harsher environment we came from. The pace is slower; the people are open and relaxed. No place to be; only being. Reality takes on a different hue when I let go of the rest of the world.

We are instructed on our second day to do something we normally wouldn't do. Joe comes up with the idea to pray. That is definitely something I wouldn't normally do. Not being sure what I believe about God makes me uncomfortable when asked to pray. Asking for help is a problem too. I pride myself on the fact that I manage my life quite well without asking for help. I'm the person other people ask for help, not the other way around. I know where my bootstraps are, thank you very much.

Joe decides a good place for us to pray is the Sanctuary, a building dedicated for meditation. We sit in the back row on floor cushions inside the silent, spacious room. I haven't a clue what to do next; praying is that foreign to me. The Sanctuary is almost empty so I feel free to get into any position that comes to mind. There are no chairs in the room; I kneel on the floor and bend over my knees with my head down. I stretch my arms out straight ahead towards the rock circle in the stone wall in front of me.

I am only in the position for a few seconds when a flood of emotional gratitude overtakes me. I start thanking God for everything in my life, my children, my home, my husband, my job, my garden tomatoes, my body, the air, and even my parents; everything comes tumbling out and the tears begin to fall. This overwhelming gratitude is completely unexpected, and surprisingly, I have no doubt to whom I am grateful. It doesn't matter that I have no idea about the nature of God or what I believe about God. At this moment I am simply grateful to be alive.

It had never occurred to me before that prayer could be devotional. That prayer may not be an avenue only to ask for something. That praying can be a vehicle to express gratitude and love. Maybe this never occurred to me because as a child I didn't feel grateful for my life.

When I was young, adults were constantly telling me I should be thankful and to stop feeling sorry for myself. That didn't work, of course; their admonishments only made me feel guilty that I wasn't grateful. Somehow that guilty feeling got mixed up in my concepts about God, but today in the Sanctuary, I have nothing but gratitude.

By the third day we are relaxed enough to sit on the floor with half the class in a lecture hall called The Lake House. When I look out any of the many windows, I see hundreds of tall, skinny, trees. On a sunny day, the light filters softly between the trees and the wind creates millions of ever-changing shadows on the ground. If it is raining out, like today, the trees offer a melancholy grace to the cloudy, misty day. Rita, a long time apprentice of Don Miguel Ruiz, the author of *The Four Agreements*, is creating a visualization of a funeral. Her hypnotic voice helps me flesh out the scene in my mind — the funeral parlor, the guests, and then the coffin with my body inside.

I imagine a typical waiting room in a typical funeral home. Dark curtains along one long wall, dim lighting, hushed voices, and flowers with sad ribbons stating the donor's sympathy. I visualize the perimeter of the room for a few moments, not willing to take the next step and look inside the coffin. Urged on by Rita's soothing and coaxing voice, I approach the front of the room to view my casket. The coffin is laid out with flowers and has mourners on both sides. The polished wooden box looms larger as I walk down the center aisle towards it. Uneasily I look over the side when I reach the velvet-covered kneeling bench directly in front of the casket.

A part of me is expecting a Chucky Doll from the popular horror movie series to pop out and send me running back down the aisle. I brace myself to jump back as I peek in over the side. There I lie, decorated with thick pancake funeral parlor make-up. The overdone rouge fails miserably in attempting to restore the glow of life in my cheeks. Dead. Without the horror, seeing my body isn't so bad. I'm still conscious; I'm only physically dead. Rita directs our attention to the people who have come to say good-bye and pay their last respects. I watch the people as they gaze inside the casket to catch a glimpse of what I once was.

I picture my children, Andrew and Garrett, saying good-bye to their mommy. I feel an ache in my heart with the thought of them growing up without me. I begin to cry; oh, how I love them! I can't stand that they are so hurt and sad and lonely and angry at my death. I want to tell them it is okay — I still love them, I have always loved them. I want to tell them not to let my dying stop them from living. I want to hold them in my arms again, but I can't. I'm dead.

I see Joe trying to comfort them while experiencing his own intense grief. I feel so bad to have left him, to not be there to help him. I want him to know I want him to be happy after this; to go on and enjoy the boys and find someone else to love and share a life with. I want him to know how much I loved being with him, creating our family together. I want him to know how much I loved him when I was alive. I see my mother and realize how much she suffers at my death. All my anger towards her dissolves in tears, and I hope she understands that I loved her more than I ever let on, especially in the last few years. I see my husband's family and continue weeping as I acknowledge how my death has saddened them. I wish I could comfort them. But I can't, I am dead.

Someone says, "What would you say to the people at your funeral if you could tell them one last thing? What would you want them to know?" My heart screams out, I love you, I love you all, and I'm sorry if I hurt you, I didn't mean to. I want them to know I love them and it is okay. I'm okay. I hear sobs all around the room and someone passes me a tissue box to use and pass on. Anthony, a big man sitting in front of me is sobbing loudly. He had told a story earlier in the workshop about his abusive father. His public sobbing is a catalyst for all of us to take this opportunity to let our hearts do the visualizing. To let our hearts feel what is really at stake when it comes to forgiveness and family.

Softly, over the sounds of sniffles and grief, I hear Don Miguel say, "Why do you wait until you are dead to tell your loved ones these things? Why?"

Slowly and gently, Rita guides us back from our internal journey to the outside reality of the Lake House. Unhurried, I drift out of my dream state, back from the dark, somber funeral home to the large, airy lecture hall. Drained, heavy, I feel the way I would have after a good, long cry when I was little. I rarely cry as an adult, but I remember now what it feels like to surrender to pure emotion with no holding back. The heaviness is akin to the settling of silt after a tumultuous storm rages through a once calm lake. The water clears, as the stirred-up sediments slowly drift to the bottom again, creating grounding and clarity out of what was recently a jar of shaken dirt and water. Weighty and settled, dense yet clear.

"Now that you are dead," Rita continues, "you are free to release all those attributes of yourself that you don't want anymore and recreate or re-dream yourself. You can die as often as you want, recreating and dreaming a new you whenever you become aware of what you want to change."

Before the funeral visualization, we had all been instructed to find a rock or a similar object that we could bury to symbolize the death and burial of our old selves. We make our way silently down the path that leads to the lake that gives the lecture hall its name, the mood somber and private.

I cup the stone in my pocket and think about where I would like my old self to be laid to rest. The thought of staying in one place in the ground seems too permanent. The water, where the current will eventually move my stone, is infinitely more appealing. Making my way to the water's edge I walk along the shore until I find a spot away from the others. I think of all the attributes I would like to leave behind in the lake. My self doubts, my fear of confrontation, my fear of standing out, my deferring nature towards people who intimidate me, my lack of boldness, my lack of spontaneity. I throw the rock in. I am surprised with the force with which I throw myself away. We had been told to be gentle with our old selves and respect where they had gotten us. But I was glad to be rid of her, the old Karyn; the Karyn trying to be like all the other Karens.

In third grade there were three Karens in my class. Back then, I wanted to be like the *y* in my name that set me apart from all the other Karens. What had changed in me since the third grade? What I wanted now was to stop needing to fit in, to stop trying to fit in. Now I wanted whatever it was that would make me feel, truly feel, happy.

Friday, the last morning of our workshop we stand shoulder to shoulder with fifty people facing another line of fifty people an arm's length away. We are gathered outside underneath a cluster of huge pine trees. The two lines of people stretch down a gentle slope to the same placid lake I threw the old me into. We are singing *I am remembering who I am* over and over as the person at the head of the line closes their eyes and walks between the two columns of people. When he or she reaches the end of the line they join in again so that the rows of people continue on until everyone has had a chance to walk through.

The ceremony is called an Angel Walk, and it is the job of the people on either side to guide the person walking through the middle with their hands. Because we have spent four days in intense intimate communications, revealing our human vulnerabilities to each other, we act fondly towards each other, even though we have just met and will most likely never see each other again.

Joe and I are facing one another. Joe looks extremely uncomfortable. He was hoping at breakfast this morning that there wouldn't be any more touchy-feely stuff today. Boy, did he get that wrong. I shrug my shoulders; there is nothing I can do for him. He is on his own. I remind myself that it was his choice to be here. I don't want to slide down that familiar path of blaming myself for someone else's discomfort.

Some on the line are patting, hugging and kissing the person as they guide them forward. Some people are held in a warm embrace before they are released and passed on. The atmosphere is thick with emotion, the ritual powerful. I watch the men and women visibly shaken as they are passed from hand to hand. Most are trembling with a hesitant joy, some are crying. Some, I think, aren't touched too often and relish the simple pleasure of another human's unconditional warmth expressed through a hand or a kiss.

As my turn draws near I become more anxious. I'm short and slightly claustrophobic, all those hands, all those strangers touching me. Some of the people are stroking the hair of the women who walk by. I cannot stand to be petted or patted on the head. The person to my right has just started her walk and I will be next — after the woman across and to the right of me. My mouth is dry, and I'm really scared now; of what, I'm not sure. Sherri, another Don Miguel apprentice, takes me in her arms and whispers reassuring words in my ear. I can't remember what she says, but I'm soothed somewhat. Sherri tells me to close my eyes, and I do; then she gently maneuvers me towards the opening. Stiff as a board, my hands visibly shaking, I reach out blindly for someone or something to guide me forward. I feel a hand grab mine, and I am so grateful for the guidance that I almost weep.

The first people to guide me are the women and men who have been standing next to me for the last twenty minutes or so. They see how tense I am and whisper additional reassurances in my ear as I pass. Some of the people further down the line stroke my hair or kiss my cheek or hug me. But to my surprise, I enjoy it. I am a little child again, hungry for a pat or a hug or a cookie. Gradually I relax. Disoriented with my eyes closed and with all the touching and chanting, I forget where I am. I keep moving along from touch to touch, slowly gaining trust in the guiding hands of warm intentions. I realize how difficult this is for me. How distrustful I am of other people's physical intent towards me. How vulnerable I feel when relying on them to guide me down the path. After what seems a very long time, I am hugged from the front, enveloped in a warm, snuggly embrace. I hear a voice whisper, "Remember, now you are married to love. Open your eyes."

Opening my eyes, I peer directly into Don Miguel's face. The daylight is so bright; I blink and behave as if I have awakened from a dream.

Confused, I say, "Oh, you are here, too, Miguel!" Surprised to see that he is holding me, I look over and see Rita and am equally surprised. I murmur, "Rita, you too?"

Up until today I had only read the books, but at Omega I live the lessons. I am blessed to be in the presence of a true spiritual leader, someone who walks the walk and can communicate the message. When Don Miguel hugs me, I am loved unconditionally. The encounter is as exquisite as it is rare.

Miguel instructs me to continue down the path with my eyes open. The difference between eyes open and eyes closed is dramatic. Having been delivered from a dark womb, I continue down the column of people in a foggy haze. With eyes open, I am able to identify the people who continue to guide me on my way. Exuberantly two people I recognize pick me off my feet and swing me around like a small child. Another hour goes by before the whole line of people finish. The Omega sound engineer, who is responsible for recording the workshop, had been so moved by the workshop that he asked to join the Angel Walk. Even he is hugged like an old friend when it is time to leave and rejoin the familiar life we briefly left behind.

Sharing vulnerabilities with people I don't know is an opening for my soul. As I exposed my hidden beliefs about myself, I began to dissolve the wall I had erected between myself and everyone else. In the enclosed, safe environment created by Omega and Don Miguel, I was able to let down my defenses and allow myself to experience my emotions as they arose. There was no need to stuff them back down or disguise them to make them more acceptable. There is freedom in letting emotions reveal themselves without judging them. Freedom in acknowledging — the good, the bad and the ugly.

The cloud of acceptance that buffered us at the Lake House evaporates on the drive home. I become exasperated with Joe when he continually asks which road is next, what is the exit number? No wonder I'm the tense one in this relationship. I fume, but he doesn't bother worrying about anything. Instead, rather than remember something as simple as directions, he asks. I'd be relaxed and easygoing too, if I didn't have to retain all this information in my head; if all I had to do was ask someone else to think for me. It isn't until we pick up the kids at their uncle's house and Andrew comments that even he knows which road is next because Mom has said it so many times, that Joe finally stops asking, and I stop being angry. Don Miguel told us we would fall back into our old dream and habits. But I wasn't ready for the fall to happen so quickly and so completely.

August 2001

When we were told that the journey toward happiness starts when you ask yourself, "What do *I* want?" with the emphasis on the *I*, I realized I didn't know what I wanted. I know what I *don't* want, but I honestly don't know what I want. I mention this fact to a friend at work, and he recommends Sonia Choquette's book, *Your Heart's Desire*. I do all of the exercises — even though I usually skip that part of self-help books. The meditation exercises are much easier than I had thought. I discover I have a knack for creating detailed visualizations. My visualizations are fascinating because they are unexpected. The images materialize spontaneously after I follow Sonia's instructions and sit silently still. Perhaps I am so unused to focusing on what is inside of me that the arising images seem foreign to my mind.

Today the most unexpected visualization emerges. I am a minister speaking to a group of spiritual seekers. The image comes up several times and I neither suppress nor encourage it. After the meditation exercise, I tell myself why this is such an improbable endeavor for me. Ministers do not make money. Ministers have lots of rules and 'shoulds'. Ministers have strict belief systems, a routine I am trying to step away from. The money aspect is a practical obstacle, and religious leadership is something I had never considered. I lay the image to rest but continue to use the book to help me in other ways.

Sonia's story of her mother inspires me to use meditation when I have problems at work or when I am undecided about an issue. Right before meditating, I throw a question I want answered out to the universe. Then I let go of the question and do not expect anything particular to happen. The important part is that I don't expect an answer or a solution. I cease putting effort into solving the problem on my own. I detach and meditate in my usual fashion by observing my thoughts and letting them go. I find that if I get out of my own way, many times an answer or a new way to look at the problem will present itself to me. The act of giving up my analytical approach to solving the problem allows a deeper perspective to emerge. Detaching from the problem takes the pressure off. Having no expectations allows for an unlimited range of possibilities. I have built a successful career being analytical. Sometimes a problem can't be solved through analysis. This new approach allows me to turn out ideas that I am not even aware I possess.

The world
stands out
on
either side

September 11, 2001

I AM ON THE CORNER OF SIXTH AND FIFTY-THIRD, SEVENTH FLOOR, PSEUDO corner office in New York City. After a morning of disbelief that gives way to horror that gives way to a surreal acceptance, I barely hold on to my ability to function in any capacity. I have the radio on in my office, while I watch streams of people make their way up Sixth Avenue to walk out of the city.

This is the day that's to become 9/11 in our history books.

Feverishly, I switch the radio station to see what else I can learn. I can't go anywhere. I cannot walk home to Long Island. *Amazing Grace* comes on, and I start to cry, cry for all that has come undone. I let my heart do the work of feeling the enormity of what has just happened. In the middle of the song, a client comes in and coolly asks for a copy of the consolidated tax return — the document is due in four days.

I apologize, put on my corporate demeanor and turn off the radio. My heart is still bleeding, but my mind takes over by habit, and I begin to get my client what she asked for. I know in the moment that I will not be working for her too much longer. No one could be asking another to work while *Amazing Grace* is playing and the world is falling down around their feet. She can't possibly be real, and I am tired of pretending not to be real with her.

11

To
live
deliberately

I'M LATE GETTING BACK FROM THE BREAK AND FIND OUT THE TEACHER HAS chosen my floor plan for group discussion — a simple drawing of my new fellowship. The congregation meets in a sanctuary that was added to the back of an old Victorian home. The house was donated to the congregation years ago, but the building does not have an aura of sacredness to me. It needs help. That's why I created a floor plan, hoping for a free consultation from my teacher, R.D. Chin, a Feng Shui Architectural Consultant.

R.D uses a Ba-Gua to point out where the building space is lacking the proper elements. The first area he points to is the office. The room needs to be realigned so the desk faces out, not inward. There needs to be organization to help bring in prosperity. The second area the teacher points out aligns on the Ba-Gua with spirituality; ironically, an empty space. Nothing is there but a walkway that leads to the double doors in front of the sanctuary foyer. The problem, according to R.D., is that the space needs to be anchored. Something heavy, a rock or a statue or a garden needs to serve as the focus for that area of the property. I can help with the office, I recently agreed to be the treasurer for our fellowship and finance is my area of expertise, but the spirituality space will require more effort. Now, at least, there is a range of possible solutions.

This is the last class of the workshop series. I almost canceled after 9/11, not wanting to be in the city any more than necessary. I found myself holding my breath when riding the subway under the East River, half expecting the lights to go out and chaos to erupt. I'm breathing easier now, like most New Yorkers, but it was tough those first weeks after the attack.

Convinced space could directly affect our moods at home, I signed up for a five-week course on Feng Shui at the New York Open Center. When Joe and I decided to knock down a wall to create a large country kitchen, simply knocking down the wall changed the energy of the room. A week after the wall came down, the builder needed to put up a sheet of plastic where the wall had been to keep out dust and dirt while work was done on the other side of the room. Even though the plastic was transparent, the energy in the room shifted again; Joe and I noticed how grouchy and hampered we felt with the plastic up. Nothing had changed on the original side of the kitchen that we were still using. But the short amount of time that the room had been opened was enough to dramatically alter the dynamic flow of energy.

R.D. has a spiritual interpretation on the use of Feng Shui. He begins each class with a meditation. He instructs us that Feng Shui focuses intent with the use of space and special objects; that much of the effect of good Feng Shui is transcendental. He tells us the practice of Feng Shui will attract positive people and bring prosperity and balance into our lives. These are elements I want in my life, and after 9/11, I know I can't take my time for granted anymore.

For me, decorating with Feng Shui is about using space to enhance what I want to demonstrate in my life. I look for energy that is productive but not hectic. Feng Shui teaches respect for ancient tradition and the wisdom of positive energy flow. For me, Feng Shui is decorating with transcendental intent.

November 2001

Joe and I are at our first gathering of a new Wisdom Group. Most of us were invited from an e-mail list started after Don Miguel's week-long workshop at Omega. After breaking into small groups of eight people, we share our beliefs about ourselves with each other. We focus on the limiting beliefs that prevent us from reaching for what we really want. A few people go first, and I decide to speak about my fear that I am unimportant, that what I secretly want will never really happen.

The group leader pushes me for the emotion I am feeling when these beliefs come up. Powerless, sad, empty are some words that come to mind. Rita, from the Omega retreat, happens to be coming towards my group at that moment and overhears me and sits on the floor next to me. She asks me to close my eyes and pretend I am about two or three years old. "What is happening?" Rita asks.

I am inhibited; acutely aware of everyone watching. I am distracted by my feelings of embarrassment and have trouble feeling anything else. I know what happened back then, but have only shared it with my therapist and one friend.

Rita asks me again, "What happened when you were two?"

This time Rita touches my right temple. I jerk from the touch and the tears start to fall. The emotion I felt as a two-year-old wells up and spills out of me. I tell the group I was abandoned by my family and left with a different family. After living with this new family, I sadly rejoin my biological family a year later.

Rita asks if I think the situation is my fault.

"No, I say, it just happened, and I couldn't do anything to stop it. I was powerless."

Rita asks if I can love that little girl and protect her and never let her be abandoned again.

"Yes, yes, I can, I can see that frightened little two-year-old, clinging to a stuffed dog all alone and scared to death. I resolve to love that little girl inside, to ease up and stop expecting that all grown up two-year-old to manage everything that comes along. To take time to comfort herself when life throws her a curve. Allow the child in this adult to heal.

"What can you do now?" Rita asks.

I remember the comment I made earlier in the day when the group was discussing self-love. I told them the story of how I had watched my then two-year-old son Andrew walk up to a mirror and kiss his reflection. What a beautiful, innocent event it was to behold. Andrew felt no self-consciousness about simply loving himself and expressing it. I contrasted that with how our society frowned upon and regarded expressions of self-love as selfish and conceited.

Growing up, I remember that one of the worst insults a girl could give another was to accuse her of being conceited. As if loving yourself without hating some aspect of yourself was a bad thing. That's how I remembered it anyway. Don't think too highly of yourself, little Miss. There were always plenty of things to hate about myself growing up — my hair, my body, my voice, my clothes, my personality, my lack of charm and on and on. I never felt accepting of myself when I was growing up.

I love the way Andrew kissed himself; maybe he would escape the horrible self-doubting, self-hating period of adolescence. I remember after Andrew toddled back to his toys, I walked up to the mirror and saw the smudge his tiny lips had left. I caught my eye in the mirror and thought, Oh, no, I can't do that. Then, oh, what the heck, as I came very close to the mirror, closed my eyes and kissed my reflection. I drew back and giggled while glancing around the room, glad I was alone except for my two self-loving children.

I open my tear-filled eyes and answer Rita's question. "I can kiss the mirror." Rita smiles back at me, gives me a hug and asks for a kiss, which I gladly give her.

An hour before midnight we gather together with almost everyone is in his or her pajamas. I can't help but think of the sixties, groupies and sex parties. I never attended such a party, but I imagine it might resemble something like this.

Our teacher gathers us around a cloth laid in the center of the floor in the main living room of the guesthouse. The room is dark except for some candles placed on tables that have been moved to the periphery of the room. She is assigning different people the task of saying a few words during the opening ceremony, and before I settle in, I hear my name called. I am asked to call in the element Air.

That's it — I can't think of anything else except, What the hell am I going to say? I don't do elements, rituals, hocus pocus or pajama parties. Already the day had been a heavy one for me with lots of tears and long unfelt emotions rising to the surface. I am comfortable enough with these people and feel free to say things I would never say to the people I know at home. But what am I supposed to say about air? I start listening to the others now that the opening ritual has begun and hope for a clue.

The people assigned to call in the sun, the moon and the four directions recite beautiful heartfelt words to seduce the spirit of these fundamental elements of nature into joining our observance throughout the night. They speak of the warmth of the sun and the illumination of the moon. They sound poetic reciting the different characteristics of the four directions and ask that these qualities be bestowed on us as we go through our soul searching tonight.

Air, air, what is like air? What can I say about air? Air is invisible, air is windy, air is ... We breathe air. Breath — I know something about breath. What does Grace, my yoga teacher, say while we are lying in Shavasana pose before beginning our breathing exercises? The voice is mine, but I hear Grace inside my head after the teacher gives me a slight nod to indicate my turn to speak. "The yogis tell us only the breath is real, all else is illusion. I ask the element of air to be with us tonight to remind us of what is real and what is illusion."

Not bad, not bad at all, for a novice, I think to myself. I relax a little, now that my big debut is over, and I try to listen to the rest of the opening ceremony. After all the candles on the makeshift altar are lit, the Mitote begins.

Joe and I are in the second of four groups that have been created by dividing up the forty people that are here for tonight's ceremony. There are eight people in our group including our group leader. She is the only one of us who has been to a Mitote ceremony before. The first group takes its place around the altar while the rest of us go to bed until we are awakened for our turn to sit. It seems like only a few minutes before I am awakened to come downstairs.

I nudge Joe awake, and we each pull a blanket around our shoulders before shuffling downstairs to meet up with the rest of our group. We enter the living room together, and I take a recently emptied seat at the altar.

Awake now and agitated, I try to resist a state of mind with which I am quite familiar. Tonight the agitation is vividly present. I am forced to listen to my thoughts, since there is nothing going on while I gaze at the pictures, crystals and sacred objects arranged before me. The agitation is caused by questions my middle age has brought about. Am I wasting my life? Shouldn't I be doing something worthwhile and making the world a better place, or am I here simply to decorate and shop?

These prosecutorial questions are followed by thoughts that affirm I am basically a good person. Then I ask myself:

Do I really need to save the planet? Isn't raising responsible, courteous children enough anymore?

I seem to find a way to rob myself of any joy in the moment by constantly condemning myself as selfish and self-centered, because I'm not doing more. More of what? I am not sure of what. A more, better me, I guess. The hamster turning the wheel in my mind is going nowhere, but in the process of going round and round, condemning and then defending, then condemning again, I see myself ruining a perfectly good life. There is no escape from my worst critic, me. I am found guilty over and over, and I resent the unfair but seemingly inevitable verdict. Why such harshness? Why do I have to defend myself from myself?

I don't belong here, I think, as I sneak a peek at the others. I am doing this wrong. Isn't this supposed to feel good? After what seems to be a long, long time, we are signaled to get up so the next group can sit down.

Joe and I take a quick bathroom break before snuggling back into our bed. I feel better when I get as close to his warm body as possible. I like the way his body heat melts the cold from my limbs as the warmth makes its way through his skin into mine.

Our next session isn't any better, but at least I feel somewhat detached from my nagging internal dialogue. Nothing I hear is new to me, but now I hear my thoughts more distinctly, as if I am overhearing a conversation between a brow-beaten child and an over-bearing parent. Yuck. What a waste of mental energy. How do I shut this off, that is the real question? I ask myself while staring into the candle flame before me.

The third and last time I sit before the altar, I am extremely tired. I didn't sleep much in between altar sittings and am now a bit punchy. I try remembering what even went on that day. I feel too drained and washed out to argue with myself anymore. I lean into the back jack I am sitting in and look up. I look straight across and into our group leader's eyes. She is beautiful. She looks angelic with the glow of the candles softly illuminating her skin and blondish curly hair. She is smiling at me, beaming really. Her whole being is beaming at me! I believe she loves me. Oh that feels soooooo good. I smile back, loving the moment, if not myself.

I remember what our teacher had said earlier in the day. She said, "What else is there to do?" Nothing I thought, there is nothing else I want to do but find out about me and how someone else can love me. I settle further into the back jack, smiling to myself, feeling trustful in this wacky place, feeling trusting of this foreign process, feeling open with these new and strangely familiar people. I feel joy seep into me like a warm liquid filling my veins.

When the next group comes down, we stay where we are. The sun is coming up, and the teacher wants to close the Mitote ceremony with everyone present. Each person who summoned an element must now release it and say a few words for the group. I am not nervous nor do I need to search for these words as I say, "I thank the element of air for helping us by showing us our illusions. I release the air knowing if we ever need to remember what happened here tonight, all we need to do is to breathe in and to breathe out."

Someone is talking when Joe and I enter our room for the last time that weekend. The voice sounds tinny, and I realize the radio is on; the alarm must have gone off while we were downstairs at the closing ceremony. I listen and realize the announcer is talking about a twelve-step program, and the step being discussed is surrender. How wonderful. How wonderful to surrender to this work, to this moment, to this self-discovery. Surrender because there is nothing else for me to do.

Faith of the larger Liberty

I STARTED READING THE BOOK ON SEPTEMBER 11TH, BUT I DIDN'T GET BACK TO it for months because of the destruction of innocent life done in the name of God that day. I remember the sick feeling in my stomach when I was told a second plane had hit the other tower, accepting that there was no possibility of an accident now. At the time, I thought about how the U.S. delegation had not liked some wording in an international document and walked out on the rest of the world. Desperate people do desperate things, I reasoned. If we don't pay attention to positive action, an international conference, for instance, we will be destined to pay attention to catastrophic deeds.

I have hundreds of memories of those few horrible days, mostly memories of hoping and wishing for more survivors. One of my cherished memories amid the dark ones occurred on the Friday after the attack. We gathered in our office lobby to listen to a prayer and have a moment of silence.

My co-workers were holding hands while a manager read a prayer that was exquisitely non-denominational. The man on my right was a Conservative Jew and the man next to him was a Pakistani Muslim. Both are devout religious observers of their faiths. After the prayer an administrative assistant broke into song with *God Bless America*. Yes, I thought, God bless America — if we can continue to respect each other as we are doing right now.

Months later, after *God Bless America* had been played and sung thousands of times and America was bombing Afghanistan my husband said, "God bless Afghanistan, they need the blessing. Those poor people have nothing." I felt blessed at the moment to be married to a man who could feel that way. Bless the Afghanis, they need blessings more then we do. Most people in my neighborhood would rather see America bomb Afghanistan off the face of the earth. God bless America so we can kill our enemies? Wasn't God the reason the terrorist gave for attacking us? Which God is the real God — our God or their God? Or is the real God my husband's God, blessing both them and us?

I am dangerously close to going back to my old conviction that religion is for fools. A powerful few, who are evil or deluded by their own twisted personification of God, use religion to manipulate the multitudes into committing extreme acts of cruelty on people who do not believe as they do. History has repeated itself so many times in exactly this way. Because of an almost universal yearning for Divine presence, a few powerful religious icons are able to affect the fate of millions by hooking people's attention and holding their beliefs with a vision of the Divine that is created with a specific agenda in mind. I wanted no part of religion then, and I didn't want it now, but there it was, literally crashing down on me and the rest of the world.

Months go by after 9/11 before I continue reading. My heart is numb from the environment of hate and fear surrounding the attack. I do not want to lose my newfound hope or give up my search for God, but I cannot reconcile my yearnings with history repeating itself yet again. Luckily, I do finish the book and the author helps explain how God is our God and their God and the God that blesses us both.

The author explains that the same God can be interpreted and experienced in totally different ways by totally different people. I always wondered why some Biblical stories of God picture him as harsh, vengeful and forever smiting enemies. God teaches hard lessons with pestilence and floods. He asks for great sacrifices and demands unparalleled, unilateral worship from his chosen followers. Other times God appears loving and welcoming, preaching forgiveness and tolerance.

Why the turn around? I wonder. What happened to God? Did he receive therapy or encounter self-knowledge through humbling traumas?

Nothing I was taught indicated anything of the sort. God is portrayed differently depending on who is telling the story.

God's image and personification is dependent on the person experiencing God. Where you are is what determines how God will be perceived by you. We will individually define God based on how we interpret our life and all of life at any given moment in time. We do this individually, as a family, as a community, as a nation and as a member of a religious community. Orthodox, Fundamentalist and Conservative religions are just that, they are static in their beliefs about God and the nature of life. That is what makes them what they are. They don't allow or encourage any changes in perception. God, and those who resist their version of God, is seen in black or white. Their mind-set does not allow growth or deviation from their stated beliefs and creed.

But if you allow yourself to evolve, God or whatever you call the Divine, will evolve with you. That is my interpretation of Deepak's opening chapters of his book, *How to Know God*. I am thrilled because I am searching for God, or more accurately, I am searching for an experience of God. This book speaks to me right off the bat.

God is what the terrorists believe him to be; God is what they live. They live as people lived in the Old Testament, surrounded by their discernible enemies. They live desperately and act desperately. The name of God is invoked to right the wrongs they believe have been done to them and their people. God is there to help them smite their enemies. The terrorist lives in survival mode — there is no forgiveness or compassion. Those qualities are not in terrorists' lives. The vast majority of the people who live in terrorist supporting nations know no justice or compassion from their own leaders or the rest of the world. They live in a constant state of flight or fight reality

For many in America, God is a God of compassion, forgiveness and love. We can afford to be compassionate, spiritually and materially. We don't have to live our lives in a fight or flight frame of mind. We have peace; have had peace for many years. We have the opportunity to achieve peace within, since we have the luxury of freedom of religion and conscience. God is what we live, how we experience life. God can be benevolent, loving and forgiving.

Our opportunity now, after 9/11, is choosing which God we want to hold onto. Do we want our experience of life in this country, our reality of a loving, forgiving God to be our guiding light or do we want to step back a level and embrace a vengeful, one-sided God who will help us smite our perceived enemies? Our opportunity, as it was after World War II with the Marshall Plan, is to help provide a life for those in the Middle East that will evolve their perception of God to an image that is closer to what we are blessed with. Will we go forward or backward after this shocking, tragic wake up call? I believe this is a global challenge for all of us. Our choices will determine how we experience life and God on this planet for centuries to come.

Find a
stillness

I ONLY HAVE A FEW MINUTES TO MEDITATE, AND I DECIDE TO ASK FOR HELP IN slowing down my reaction time at work. I specifically ask for help in maintaining a gap, a gap between when I am aware of a situation and my reaction to that situation. Year-end is a hectic time at work and earnings per share for the world-wide consolidated group of companies cannot be calculated until the tax department is done with their calculations and journal entries.

Last year the tax numbers were not due until April, this year they are due February 11th. The new software is my responsibility, and I need to make sure everyone can use it properly and are able to get their work done on time.

The tax server, shared by eleven people, is failing. The software vendor does not know if hardware or software is causing the problem. I troubleshoot the problem over the phone with client support for six hours — until a specialist shows up — then continue for another six hours with the specialist on the premises. All the while no one can access or use the program. The tax department is shut down.

Before today I would have been sharp and unforgiving with anyone who came within a three-foot radius of me. I would have attempted to control the situation by trying to control the behavior of everyone around me while dishing out the blame to everything and everyone. Today I allow the situation to unfold without taking anything personally and reserve judgment as much as possible. It doesn't matter that the software company may have screwed-up; what matters is that it gets fixed. It will get fixed, or not, regardless of whether I make myself crazy. It will get fixed, or not, regardless of whether I take someone's head off for a lost day at this critical time.

I amaze myself with my ability to stay calm and watch the day unfold without beating myself up or blaming anybody else for the stressful situation. Today I realize how asking for help, even if I don't know who or what I am asking help from, is a real benefit to me and to those around me.

March 2002

This is the morning I realize my mind is not strictly my own. That there are those who walk the earth and have the ability to slip through the thin membrane that provides enough smoke to cause us to believe we are separate from God and each other. It is the morning when I am allowed a glimpse of an existence that is foreign, yet available to me. An existence of freedom and starlight. My first Dreaming session proves to be a metaphor for the unfolding of the next two years of my life.

I start out on a beach and end up with the stars. I am not alone; my guide on this journey is with me. How, I do not know, but his presence is unmistakable. I receive a gift, a preview; a return of awe that this life is best lived with. The vision forever changes my view of reality, consciousness and God. The encounter is new, exceptional, and I feel ill-equipped to communicate the experience to the group. I write it down instead. The dream turns out to be the first of three incredible journeys I will come upon this weekend in New Jersey.

After lunch I am chosen to be one of four women to participate in a ritual. We lie down in the middle of the circle, one woman for each direction, our heads touching in the center and our legs pointing out towards the others like spokes of a wheel. Four men are asked to sit between the women. Everyone else stays in their dreaming chairs. Someone begins singing from the corner of the room.

I feel acutely vulnerable and openly intimate with my head touching another's while lying flat on my back with thirty other people looking on. I was picked out of the crowd, and, like a little kid in elementary school, I've been asked to do something special for my favorite teacher. I am excited — and nervous, unable to fade back and be part of many. I see myself from my suburban soccer mom point of view and feel ridiculous. What am I, some doddering, old hippie type looking for a drugless thrill? I throw away that perspective immediately; aware that such thoughts will ruin any insight or fun I might gain from the odd situation I have deliberately put myself in.

Our teacher asks those of us in the center to send out to the others in the circle. I don't know what that means, and — so I imagine water flowing from me to the outside circle. I imagine the water filling up chalices they hold in their hands. The water spills over and flows back down to the center to mix with the water there and cycles back to the circle again, overflowing and recycling in a constant moving connection between us. The water is golden, sparkling in a sunlit sort of way. I am surrounded by golden water while I purposefully will the water to flow from the center to the outer rim of the circle. My belief that people need to be filled up before they can begin to love and nurture others creates this image. I visualize filling them up with love and the medium of water is what comes to me.

I hear a song about ancient volcanoes. I try to imagine a mountain, but see a pyramid instead. I go with what is presented in my mind's eye and visualize a scene from Egypt — and a Sphinx appears in the distance. The blustery March wind is blowing outside as a desert wind blows sand across the stone monuments.

My perspective changes, and like the first dream I experienced this morning, I am aware of watching and participating rather than directing the vision. The wind becomes terribly strong and begins to dissolve the pyramids and Sphinx as if it is being worn away from thousands of years of erosion. Breathlessly, I turn my head to see a huge tree with its leaves being stripped by the wind, then it too dissolves as day turns into night.

"Don't be afraid, don't be afraid," I say repeatedly to the people sitting silently around me as hundreds of thousands of years slip through my mind in seconds. The piles of sand that were the pyramids are blown away with the wind, and nothing but space and stars and darkness remain. I no longer feel the floor beneath me or walls surrounding me. One part of me is hanging on for dear life, while another part of me projects out to the group the thoughts that enter my head as soon as I become aware of them. *"Don't be afraid, there is no dying, you are the light and the dark, you are both."*

The frenzied pace of the dream slows, and I am looking down from above. I see a pool of still, dark water. I tell everyone to look, and we do. What we see are stars reflected in water. I tell them to go into the water and look up and see the stars through the water. We gaze from under the water up into the sky and see the same star-filled dark night that we saw reflected in the pool a moment before. When the singing stops the vision of stars falls away and the connection to the rest of group fades, my heart slows to a steady beat. But I don't move.

I am awestruck by the vision, the message, and the connection. Where did the images come from? What is going on? I don't have a clue. The feeling of expansion and infinity is truly mind-blowing. I can only guess I have tapped into an ancient mystery somehow. Maybe someone out there or in me or both is trying to tell me — us — something? But what? If I believe what I projected, immortality exists, and we are all made of the same stuff as space and stars. We are the dream, and the dream is us, and we replicate what is reflected through us. The endless cycle of consciousness creating reality, reality evolving consciousness, consciousness creating reality . . .

Unlike the last Mitote ceremony, when my words seemed absolutely perfect for summoning the element of air, I don't have any inspiring words when the teacher picks me to call forth the four-legged creatures later that night. After the lighting of the altar, we are instructed to look for our hands in our dreams when it is our turn to sleep.

Hoping for sleep, Joe and I find our way to our makeshift sleeping quarters. For the Mitote ceremony to run smoothly, everyone in the same group must be sleeping near each other, so that we can be summoned easily when it is our turn to sit by the altar. Since Joe and I were originally sleeping in another building, we had to create a bed out of futons and sleep in the den which is adjacent to the living room where the altar is set up. All of our group members are sleeping together in the den, so I am careful moving around the crowded room. Some people are on couches, some on the floor in sleeping bags and others are sleeping on futons like us.

I don't want the ceremony to be a bust and am apprehensive because I want something good to happen. But I don't want to set up any expectations either. I know I have killed many a good time by having expectations of what should happen. My mind starts to run — that little hamster wheel inside my head, round and round, no beginning or end, just endless, useless turning of thoughts.

Well, I tell myself, don't expect anything. But what do I want? I hear myself ask. I want peace, peace of mind, I tell myself in a definitive, internal voice. Soon after, I drift off to sleep with Joe's deep, steady breathing next to my ear.

Someone taps me on my shoulder. I awaken to the unfamiliar scene of near strangers rubbing their eyes as they clumsily get to their feet in their pajamas. I poke Joe and he wakes up with a confused look on his face. We lift our still sleeping bodies to a standing position and follow the others to the living room. *Om Namaha Shivaya* chanting drifts quietly out of the room as I enter. The group of people before us gets up as we enter the room. We glance briefly at each other as we exchange places surrounding the makeshift altar on the floor. The room is dark, except for the candles on the floor. The altar is filled with personal items people have placed around the candles, flowers and incense. I settle into a back jack and look around. Some people have already closed their eyes, some are gazing into the candlelight. We recite a prayer and then fall into our silent meditations.

As I settle in, I become aware of the music again. After a few rounds of the chant, I recognize the words from a Kundalini yoga class I had gone to several weeks ago. In the yoga class the chant was repeated for seven minutes while I sat cross-legged with arms up over my head, palms pressed together, a posture that opens the heart area. The Kundalini instructor had asked the students to meditate on what they were grateful for in their lives while they chanted *Om Namaha Shivaya*. During the chant, I was brought to tears thinking of my children, home, husband, family, food, everything. I had been so overwhelmed by the emotion of gratitude that I had to stop chanting and compose myself. I hadn't wanted to make a spectacle of myself in yoga class. But something about the chanting and the posture allowed me to feel gratitude for everything that day. The feeling wasn't limited to thank you for this, but not for this other, unpleasant part of my life. There was only a total outpouring of gratefulness. The emotion had come forth powerfully and unbidden, like many I was experiencing lately.

Sitting at the Mitote altar, in the middle of the night, hearing the same chant, I submit to the same outpouring. In a meditative pose, the tears start streaming down my face. I start thanking every person, every situation and every action that has gotten me to this place at this moment. I thank Grace, my yoga teacher, my mother, my children, Joe, my boss, my crazy childhood, my father, my crappy jobs — everything.

I can only feel the magnitude of how all the events and people in my life conspired to bring me here tonight, sitting in a candle lit room with incense, crying for the wonder that is my life. I realize nothing has changed in my life, since I started my spiritual quest. But what I feel and experience in life is completely different. I see the difference the same as comparing the rich deliciousness of actually *tasting* a spoonful of warm hot fudge and cold vanilla ice cream in my mouth and trying to recreate the sensation of a hot fudge sundae with my mind. That is the difference I am experiencing in my life right now. Feeling life, not thinking it.

After my turn at the altar, before I fall back asleep, I feel myself swaddled in a field of fluffy white. I look at my hands before drifting off to sleep, but I do not find them in my dreams. Too soon I am awakened again. The rest of my group and I stumble to our feet and make our way back to the altar. I don't want to close my eyes this time or maintain a straight back for a correct meditative posture. I relax into the back of my seat and lazily look at the objects in front of me.

A man from the previous group is in the corner of the room with three women around him. They are all Reiki practitioners, placing their hands in various positions around his body. One woman is chanting as well as focusing healing energy towards the man's upper body. She has a good voice, but the chanting seems loud in comparison to the usual quiet of the Mitote ceremony. The position of the women's arms looks difficult to hold, but they never waver or lower their arms while soothing whatever ails the gentleman they are healing.

I watch the scene with calm detachment. The chanting in the corner would normally have disturbed me, but for some reason I am unperturbed by the commotion. I am strangely at ease with the unfamiliar scene. After a few minutes of sitting and gazing, I realize I am not thinking about anything. There is no internal dialogue jabbering away inside my head, as if someone has turned off a radio that only tuned in stations with static. The peace and quiet inside my mind is blissful. No voice telling me what I should be feeling right now, no voice telling me I am a fool for sitting up in the middle of the night with strangers reciting prayers and lighting candles. Nothing — no commentary.

I continue to lazily gaze at the candlelight. Once in awhile I look up at the faces of the people around the altar. Curious about what they are experiencing but not curious enough to formulate any thoughts about it. Ten minutes later, the chanting stops and the women move the gentleman into another room to rest. The additional quiet only increases my sense of well-being and peace. Nowhere to go and no place to be takes on a new meaning for me. Sitting and being is as full an experience as I could ever ask for. In fact, it is exactly what I had asked for tonight before going to sleep. Peace is what I had asked for; how blessed to receive it.

I look at my hands again before falling asleep for the third time. Again I am awakened after what seems like only minutes. Joe looks even more dazed and confused than before. A middle aged man from Westchester looks like he is sleepwalking. The rest of our group is disheveled and disoriented, which I guess, is the whole point. We take our places for the third and last time. I notice that there is a storm outside. The wind is blowing, and wind chimes tinkle loudly nearby. I sit with my eyes two-thirds of the way closed and go into a semi-meditative state. Relaxed but no longer sleepy, my mind begins to gently wander. I wonder how the ritual was put together. I think about the different people who had come this time. Some were Toltec associates of Don Miguel and a few of the assistants had not been at the previous Wisdom Group weekend.

I wonder how the organizers decide who to invite. I intuit that the ceremony and the weekend is made up in the moment. They are creating it spontaneously. That is the whole point — to create! The whole week-long workshop with Don Miguel was about creating my life and my happiness. That is what the teacher is doing with these weekends and with her life. At that moment the wind blows and a sound of medieval wooden horns pierces the quiet night; an exclamation point to my epiphany. I grasp that I am also creating the weekend — I created this scene, this celebration and these people.

I open my eyes fully and look at the people sharing my reality of the moment. Halfway around the circle, I notice Robert. He is sitting with his arms wrapped around his knees, his blanket pulled completely over his head with only a small opening for his mouth and nose. I see E.T. Robert looks just like E.T. did when Elliot hid him in a blanket and flew off with him on his bicycle to escape the well intentioned but deadly government agents.

I laugh at myself, thinking, Who else would have come up with this scene? I understand clearly that I create these people by how I interpret and react to them. The reality of them is created by my perception of them. It is embedded in my point of view at any given moment. I realize that the more I like and accept myself, the more I am able to like and love the people sitting here tonight; they are projections of myself and can only reflect back what I put out there.

I think of the wonderful Christmas I had created last December. How after so many disappointing childhood holidays, I finally created the day I had always dreamed of as a child. You can do this! I tell myself. Create a beautiful life. I have already accomplished it with one day and in many other moments. I understand the art of creating my life. I know my life will only reflect back to me what I project out from my inner world. Self-love is the beginning of a beautiful life. I am certain — I see clearly the result of my inner calm and acceptance.

Sunday morning I motion a friend over to the empty seat next to me. Our chairs are arranged in a circle again. I feel as emotionally close to her as I do to the family with whom I grew up. I feel more comfortable telling my friend, a Reiki master, my spiritual tales than I would my family. The cynical edge and analytical approach to life isn't there with her. I find it comforting to be able to speak with another and have everything I say accepted. Accepted — because she, too, is experiencing events she can not explain and never expected. Like me, her past had nothing in it to prepare her for the strange and marvelous happenings of the last few months.

The weekend has been an introduction to Dreaming and to the concept of I AM. The lectures and ceremonies are to facilitate our becoming aware of our beliefs and how they keep us trapped in a negative self-image which, in turn, creates negative, self-limiting habits. The first Wisdom Group weekend was about the tools used to uncover these beliefs. Now that these beliefs are being discovered, this weekend we are dreaming to find out the I AM, now that we, hopefully, no longer believe the I am NOT.

Our teacher starts us off. She asks us to dream the 'I AM,' and if you can't do that, she urges us to dream gratitude, an attitude that will cultivate positive feelings. There is no music this time and very little guidance. Intimidated, I sit with eyes closed, imagining . . . what? Rescuing me from confusion, the teacher suggests continuing on the theme of last night's Mitote. At the end of last night's Mitote ceremony, I was positive about my ability to create a beautiful life. My gratitude for my life was especially strong last night, and that feeling seems to be a good place to start my dreaming.

Visualizing is difficult. There is no location from which to start. During the dreaming session before, there had been someone singing; that elicited distinct images for me. This time I am on my own. I begin by imagining I am in a forest, walking alone through the trees. As I walk I create more depth to the imagery in my mind. I hear the crunch of fallen leaves underneath my feet. I see mist off in the distance and notice sunlight filtering through the tree branches. After a moment or two of fleshing out my dreamscape, I hear music coming from far away in the forest. I am aware the sound is only in my dream and not in the physical room in which I am sitting. I stop walking and concentrate on listening to the music in the distance. As I concentrate, the melody becomes slightly louder. Vaguely familiar, I reminisce on the times I would hear a song on the radio, and after the first few bars, try to identify the song before the singer started singing.

As the music gets louder, I recognize the vibrations of an electric guitar. The notes of the song ring more distinctly as the melody floats through the trees towards me. I strain to recognize the tune. A little closer, a little louder, and I have it. *I am a Warrior* by Joan Jett and the Blackhearts! I freak out a bit but stay with the dream. I AM a warrior. Yes, yes, that's what I am, a WARRIOR! Again, the dream has taken on a life of its own. At some point I cease to be the director, and become the protagonist and observer at the same time. The warrior mantle suits me. I have at different times in my life taken on Goliath. Nothing epic, but I have taken on the stance of a warrior. I have a measure of fearlessness when it comes to authority, especially when

I think authority is bullying. I am willing to do battle and had done so in the past.

I am back in the director's seat of my dream and imagine myself walking in the forest again, but this time with a bow and arrow. I am dressed as I imagine the Goddess Diana would be dressed in Mythical times. I am a warrior, a Dream Warrior. A Dream Warrior? Yes, this is something I'm good at. Three incredible dreams the first time out of the gate.

I enjoy envisioning myself strong and capable. What is my purpose as a dream warrior? I ask myself. I walk on and see a large tree in the distance. There are huge balls hanging from the upper branches. I draw back my bow and shoot an arrow into the ball; it explodes into a thousand tiny lights. The lights stay illuminated as they are carried by an unfelt wind throughout the forest. And I know I am not a warrior to battle against others but to battle darkness. My weapon of choice is words. I will spread light with words. This is the message of my dream.

Kum
ba
yah

OMEGA'S *HEART OF HAPPINESS* CONFERENCE IS BEING HELD IN A HOTEL A BLOCK
and half from where I work. The brochure lists so many authors of
books I have read I have difficulty choosing which workshops to attend.
Carolyn Myss is giving a full day seminar the day before the conference.
I am here today to hear her speak for the second time. The first time I
sought her out was because her first book, *Anatomy of Spirit* created
an opening in my life.

Carolyn's book explained that to free my spirit and to find my spiritual
path, I must break free of the beliefs that my family and culture had
imposed on me as a child. I need to challenge whether I really believe
what I was taught and determine whether the belief is more habit than
faith. If I discover I don't believe what has been imposed on me, then
that does not mean *nothing* exists for me; it means I need to find out
for myself what is true.

Once I realized that I didn't have to abandon the idea of God because
I didn't agree with any religious beliefs that had been presented to me
so far, a space was created in my mind for the possibility of a different
God. This small space was all that was needed.

I didn't find God, God found me — on the Long Island Railroad, of
all places. One day after changing trains at Jamaica station, I squeezed
by and settled into an awkwardly intimate seat, forced to face people
with our knees almost touching. I felt the invisible boundaries go up
around each individual body. We all need that illusionary piece of turf

we consider our personal space. New Yorkers are incredibly civilized considering how often their small bit of space is compromised. Simply getting to work in the morning is an exercise in civility. I wonder how many howdy-dos those cordial southerners would be exchanging if they had a commute like mine every day. Polite silence is the height of New York civility, and I, for one, was grateful for it.

Nearing the end of *Anatomy of Spirit,* I read about the paradox of going through the pain of being responsible for all your decisions, all your beliefs, all your actions, and then surrendering, because in the end, you have no control. This is not the same as pre-destination, the author explained. Our choices and beliefs determine our reaction to life, how much we enjoy life — or not. Ultimately, wrote Carolyn, we must surrender to a higher order, something not quite comprehensible to humans. Her philosophy reminded me of twelve-step programs. They promote personal responsibility while surrendering to a higher power.

About ten minutes from my final destination, a passage from the book triggers the image of my angel picture at home. As the image of my angel came to mind, I had an overwhelming desire to kneel and bow my head to the floor in front of the angel. The feeling of surrendering to God was overwhelming. The urge was so genuine, so deep, and so unexpected that I was at a loss about what to do. I could have dropped to my knees and sobbed with a release of tension I didn't know I was carrying, but the train was packed and there was no place to hide or pray or fall apart. Instead I kept my head down, wiped away my tears and blew my nose. The image of me kneeling in front of an angel was emblazoned in my mind's eye; yet surrender is a foreign notion to me. Since my teenage years, I have resolutely held my autonomy as being of the utmost importance. Being at the helm of my own life is a driving force and surrender to anyone or anything is not an option for me. I never bowed before the angel — I wouldn't allow it. But that day on the train I became aware that some part of me yearned for unity with God.

I want to experience the Divine personally again but am no longer willing to let anyone else define God, spirit, purpose or a religious practice for me. I have experienced God personally because I created a space within myself for that to happen. I know self-esteem is key to my spiritual awakening; I need to love myself enough to not deny the gift waiting to be given.

Carolyn's seminar delivery is lively, and she doesn't pull any punches. No coddling from Ms. Myss. She invites her listeners to be totally honest and take responsibility for their beliefs and choices in life. The filled lecture room falls silent when Carolyn points out the contradiction of wanting to experience God directly, while at the same time being terrified of what that will do to our comfortable life — that our cultural perception of a spiritual person is associated with the saintly qualities of being celibate, alone, poor and totally self-sacrificing. So the desire and the fear of finding God are equally present for most people.

Carolyn holds herself up as an example of a spiritual person that proves our conceptions wrong or, at the very least, narrow. She is in a relationship, happy, well off and enjoys material things. But, she also points out; she works hard and has transformed her way of being. To realize your divine potential may not be easy, she tells us, but it doesn't necessarily mean the end of earthly pleasures either.

We want to know God; but we are afraid to know God at the same time. We resist — believing we have control. We create hundreds of habits to give ourselves the illusion we have control. We don't. We only have choices, and our life is created by our choices. So, I want to know God but am afraid to know God at the same time. What if the Divine wants me to do something I don't want to do? What if it means I won't see my family? What if reaching my potential is uncomfortable or painful? I love feeling the Divine in my life, but do I really want to *change* my life? I've worked so hard to feel good about where I am. I enjoy creating a physical environment that provides a warm, spacious, beautiful place to be; I like shopping for *stuff*. I'm afraid to lose any of it. She is right. I am afraid and yearning at the same time. What do I do?

The next morning's workshop is for pleasure only. Tom Robbins, a not necessarily spiritual author, is the guest speaker. His irreverent take on the world was a beacon of light during my struggle to conform in a material world during my twenties. I wanted things. I believed I needed to conform to make the money I needed to buy the things I wanted. I was building the security I didn't even realize I craved. What a joy it was to come home and read his humorous, evocative, delightful word winding tales of non-conformist characters.

The person who introduces Tom Robbins explains that he rarely accepts speaking engagements. She has been trying for years to get him to speak at one of Omega's conferences, and this is the first time he has said yes. He speaks about language, his love and livelihood and how words, especially spoken words, can be interpreted many different ways. He illustrates by telling us that JFK's famous line "I am a Berliner" could also be translated into "I am a Jelly Donut." How different history would have been if that had been the spin the media gave to JFK's speech.

The presentation is a symphony of alliterations, humor and wit. At the end of his talk the moderator tells us Tom will take questions from the audience. A woman with a portable microphone goes from one raised hand to another as loyal readers try to take advantage of prying into this ingenious and elusive man's mind. I can't think of a single thing to ask; I am simply grateful to be here — to meet a person whose work I have enjoyed for so many years.

Thank him and let him know how much you appreciated his creation, pops into my head. Acknowledging the thought, I tell myself, yes, I will do this. Scanning the room I spot the young woman with the microphone. I know she will come to me, even though there are at least two hundred other people in the room. Her back is to me as she waits for the person asking a question to finish. As I focus on her with my full intent of thanking Tom Robbins, she turns around and looks straight at me, then nods to indicate that I will be next.

The moderator on stage says she will take one more question; twenty hands go up to join the ten already in the air. I know before the woman with the microphone turns around, that she will come to me. I stand up as she ignores the many people vying for her attention as she makes her way across the room to me. When she hands me the microphone the moderator again says this will be the last question.

"I don't have a question," I say, as I look up at Tom Robbins. "I wanted to thank you for *Jitterbug Perfume*." He takes off the sunglasses he has been wearing all morning and looks me in the eye. He appears genuinely touched and humbled by my gratitude and simply says, "You're welcome." Everyone stands and applauds Tom and his work — his work that values the quest for freedom of thought and speech in a unique way. For him to be touched and to have set it up so perfectly is exhilarating.

I knew. I *knew* before I raised my hand that I would be able to thank this man for his gift to us. I am more certain of this then I have ever been about anything. I knew it would happen. I made it happen. If only I knew how I did it! Was it synchronicity, focused intent, overwhelming gratitude? Was the encounter all of that and perhaps something more?

That afternoon, I still can't get Carolyn's lecture out of my mind. I can't let go of the conflict I feel about the spiritual awakening I am in the middle of. Alive and excited, I continue to resist the urge to surrender. I am searching but don't know where the search will lead me or whether I am prepared for what lies ahead.

Dropping into an overstuffed leather chair in the hotel lobby, I decide to take Carolyn's advice and give up the illusion of control. I obviously don't have it; all I have is the ability to choose at any given moment what to do. I am responsible for the choices in my life, and how I choose to interpret what is happening around me. But I do not have control. I can steer the boat and avoid a sand bar, but I have no control over whether there are rapids up ahead. I find it easier to accept this than to continually attempt to protect myself from what may come to pass. That is not living — that is worrying. Doing so doesn't accomplish anything but angst. I wish to choose in the moment, be responsible for that choice and let go.

The next workshop is a gamble. I wasn't sure what to take and signed up for Lynda Barry's *Writing the Unthinkable*. I'm not interested in writing anything besides Julia Cameron's recommended morning pages. My life is so full I can't even imagine writing more than three pages a day.

The accumulated handouts from the previous workshops makes my shoulder bag heavy, so I arrive early and spot a seat in the second row near the aisle. A sweater and writing pad have been placed on the aisle seat. Usually I like the comfort of an empty seat next to me but decide to sit next to the occupied seat. The space factor at this conference is definitely more intimate than any other I've attended. Even New Yorkers' comfort zones seem much more relaxed this weekend.

I dig my notebook out from under all the accumulated conference paraphernalia and wait for the teacher to arrive. My absent neighbor sits down, and I know I have seen her someplace else and try looking at her without being too obvious. I tell her she looks familiar and ask if she has been to the Oaks for the Wisdom Group weekends.

"Yes!" she says. "I thought you looked familiar, too."

She is so full of energy and life that I wonder why she is going to happiness seminars. She tells me she is a personal coach and uses what she learns here to help her clients. I can see she would make an excellent personal coach. Her energy is contagious.

Lynda Barry enters the room; we stop chatting and turn to the front. The teacher doesn't sit; instead she paces back and forth in front of the class in a manic fashion. She tells us about herself in a hilariously self-deprecating manner. She puts us at ease as she presents a stepping stone method to writing memories. She demonstrates an example and gives us a category to try ourselves.

We bend our heads over our pads and start writing. Unexpectedly the words come easily. Who thought writing about a car could bring back so many memories? But it works; in forty-five minutes we are laughing *and* writing.

Lynda is the funniest teacher of any kind I have ever had. She tells us she is going to be at Omega in the summer for a weeklong seminar.

I lean over to my neighbor and say, "Can you imagine a week with her? What a blast!" She agrees and gathers her things. We say goodbye, expecting to see each other again at a Wisdom retreat. As it turns out, I never see her again, but I do set my intent to attend Lynda's weeklong workshop at Omega this summer.

The following morning I examine my control issues and see how I still cling to the illusion that I somehow contribute to keeping my life safe from calamity. I edge towards giving up the illusion of control. I resist surrendering. I believe the bargaining I began is what is causing my uneasiness right now. I feel the need to create, and I can't deny this calling. Calling to what I don't know. God or the universe will have to clue me in sometime. I need to check it out and stop bargaining or making conditions and imposing controls that I don't have anyway. I have struggled most of my adult life to gain control of my life, and it is hard to let go of that illusion. I have a wonderful life; I don't want the universe fucking it up. But I don't have control, not really. I'm not going to be happy until I follow my heart, surrender, and open up to the possibilities the universe may provide.

Outside my kitchen window the magnolia buds are out, giant purple pods of life. The daffodils have popped. The cherry tree in front is blooming. Oh wonderful springtime! I have to decide what I am going to do today. I have to re-pot the clematis, and I should transplant my herbs and turn over the garden bed. Wednesday I can buy lettuce and beans and plant the garden and put the pansies in my flowerpots on the fence. I have to finish the Sunday bulletin and call World Mission Craft. I want to make sure I spell everything right in my first service announcement.

April 2002

There is no money for this. Sounds intriguing, but I really don't have the money for this. Allie, my career counselor has recommended the conference twice now, and has even gotten me a fifty percent discount. But I can't afford it. Forget about paying for the conference, I won't get paid on the day I miss work. Eight billable hours is eight billable hours. But it sounds so interesting:

Spirit in Business, Ethics, Mindfulness and the Bottom Line.

Wouldn't it be fantastic to work for a company that actually promoted that! Hell, I'd settle for working for a company whose CEO believed in that. I don't know — I wish Allie had never brought it up. I am always pushing the envelope, going to extremes when I find something new that I like. I'd never been to a spiritual workshop ever until this year, and now this will be the fifth one. If I go. I don't know. I really can't afford it.

The Hunterspoint Ave. train gets me in early with a subway that comes by every three minutes. When I pause to cross the street to catch the number 7, I look up. Having worked in New York City for over eighteen years, I rarely look up anymore. I do this morning and stare at the word SPIRIT in huge letters on a billboard directly above and to the left of me.

Momentarily stunned, I blink and look around to see what is going on. Someone had put up a billboard for a new movie called *Spirit — Stallion of the Cimarron.* I spot a cartoon horse occupying the rest of the billboard. I didn't even notice a billboard here before. I didn't come to any conclusions about attending the conference on the way in, but this settles it. I never make decisions for ridiculous reasons like this. I'll go, and for today, believe I am getting signals from . . . who knows what?

* * *

It is an odd conference and at first the mix of business and spirit has a dissonant ring to me. Can I take the business people who attend spiritual conferences seriously? Are they here to find a job? Why would a successful businessperson be here? And, if you are truly a spiritual person, what are you doing at a business conference? I don't know anyone except Allie, and graciously, she introduces me to two friends she has hooked up with. After a rough start, with myself, that is. I have a tendency to beat myself up when I'm not as witty and outgoing as I believe I should be; I allow myself the luxury of absorbing the conference as a whole experience and stop expecting any concrete results from my investment of time and money.

A woman police chief from India explains how she enrolled the police force in a ten day Visspassana meditation retreat. Her intent was to create mindfulness in the police officers. A situation will less likely escalate into violence if the authority figure is not simply reacting to a potential criminal but is fully mindful of his or her own actions.

I like the fact that the police chief is doing something concrete with the practice of meditation. I happen to sit down next to an older gentleman that looks like he shops at Brook Brothers. We start up a conversation, and I find out he has gone to a Visspassana Meditation retreat and is planning to go again. He tells me the retreat changed his life. There is no stiffness in his demeanor as he promotes the benefits of the intense and concentrated method of meditation the Visspassana retreat offers. My preconceived notions of Indian women are blown away with the police chief, and now a person who looks to be a conservative Republican businessman is talking to me about meditative transformation.

Each day of the conference we breakout for Appreciative Inquiry sessions. Appreciative Inquiry is a method of getting a group to work together to solve business problems. The dynamics are stimulating as we interact, create and listen to each other. We brainstorm ways for business to bring forth spiritual results while still making a profit. We demonstrate how mindfulness can be used in a business setting. We joke, share experiences and laugh. Business people who can talk about business and their spirituality in the same sentence are refreshing.

On the last day I meet a young man who works for American Express. He had taken a five-month sabbatical at Omega and used what he learned to influence the business decisions of top executives where he works. American Express is one of the corporate sponsors of the conference and one of their top executives was a keynote speaker.

I had assumed anyone who is in the corporate world has no spiritual side. I am bowled over by the amount of successful business people who really do care about bringing spirit to business and not making a business out of spirituality. I feel so full of hope and love when it is time to go, I give my gentleman friend from the Visspassana presentation a hug and a kiss goodbye. I couldn't leave without sharing my heart with someone.

The *Spirit in Business* mood stays with me. I want to do something to spread the word, to share not only my heart, but what I am experiencing. Standing in the kitchen I acknowledge my desire to write a book that changes the way people think about God and religion, and our place in the world. I laugh at myself with a large dose of love. Why not dream big!

A few days later, driving on Sunrise Highway, a title for a book springs forth, *Findings from the Hunting Party's Scout*. I'm the scout. Everyone else is in the hunting party. We are all hunting our spiritual selves, searching for the life force that animates us. Sometimes people don't even know they are searching — and the search ends tragically in alcoholism or drug addiction. Sometimes the search leads to isolation, deprivation and self-sacrifice as depicted by the lives of saints, nuns and monks. But the search doesn't have to end up like that. My journey is proof and I want to report back what I find. Let everyone know this isn't all there is. Just keep hunting.

April 29, 2002

My first service was a great success for World Mission Craft and me. By eleven twenty the sanctuary was full. I wasn't nervous in the least. I enjoyed the view and position from the pulpit. Erve graciously agreed to play piano, and that kept the program flowing nicely. Laura added an ending with a reading that was perfect. The Eckhardts were excellent speakers and well prepared. They did a wonderful presentation of World Mission Craft and its goals of providing self-supporting work for Third World nations. Everyone present participated and bought lots of hand made African artwork, instruments, jewelry, and kitchen utensils. It was a good day, a great beginning.

Lighting
the Chalice

My friend Patti says a person wearing boots feels like they can kick some ass.

I'm wearing cowboy boots on the journey to France. Yoga pants, cowboy boots and a stylish black and white top from Ann Taylor topped off with a black leather jacket and black Varnet sunglasses, Jackie O size; feeling good, animated and surprisingly grounded. Maybe it is the boots; they always lend me a sense of authority. I am more solid, less wishy-washy in my boots. Confident that I am where I am supposed to be. I can't believe I'm here in Southern France touring sacred sites with nine people I don't know because of a workshop I took less then a year ago.

Walking to our first sacred site we pass a rustic tavern with horses tied to a wooden rail outside. Apparently the boots were a good choice. We pose for a picture so we can tell the folks back home we rode into town. Every year gypsies flock to St. Marie de la Mer to honor Sarah. One legend claims Sarah was a servant of Mary Magdalene and came to France with Magdalene and Mary, the mother of Jesus. The three women supposedly came across the Mediterranean Sea from Egypt in a boat and landed in France. Other legends claim Sarah is Mary Magdalene's daughter and Mary's granddaughter. No matter which legend is believed, there is no question that the gypsies venerate Sarah.

Our dreaming guide, one of the trip's organizers, brings us to a simple chapel that dates back to the ninth century. Inside the sanctuary is a statue of the two Marys in a boat. Underneath the altar is a crypt alcove, lit by hundreds of candles. As the long, thin candles melt, they become wavy, dripping spirals, leaving the crypt an absent Dracula ambiance. The alcove is overly warm; there are candles in every nook and cranny, and the low arched roof traps the heat. A statue, which I assume is Sarah, is in one corner with a line of people waiting to get close. Uncomfortable waiting in line with the faithful, I watch them kneel, say a prayer or cross themselves as they pay homage to Sarah.

When close enough, I am amazed to see that Sarah is a child. Sarah is a black child with a sweet face and slightly turned up lips. She is decorated in layers of clothes; an oversized doll that a little girl has overdressed. I have a strange desire to comfort Sarah; it seems an awfully big obligation to fulfill the hopes and dreams of so many worshipers. She is only a baby, I murmur, as I leave the sacred space.

Back in the main service area Joe and I sit down in one of the pews. Our guide invites us to dream for a few minutes. This will be my first time dreaming in a public place. Before I close my eyes I look around and take in my surroundings. The worshipers making their way past the two Marys and down the steps to Sarah's crypt are predominantly women.

I begin dreaming — and a sudden swelling of compassion for these women overtakes me. I feel their need to be included in the ceremony of faith. That is why they are here. This place honors the feminine; the pilgrimage gives voice and space to express the desire to worship the Divine Feminine. The normal, formal religious services do not create such an atmosphere. The priest or minister is at the head, interpreting, leading the congregation. The faithful are kept at arms' length from the full expression of devotion. These people, these women, need to participate to come fully into their own experience of God. Sitting here watching the flow of devotees, I realize I want to help. I want to be a champion for these women. I want to be that Dream Goddess Warrior who helps bring down the crusty, exclusive, patriarchal religious services and replaces them with services designed to inspire every individual's unique celebration of divinity and love.

A few days later, Joe gives out the gifts he brought from New York for the tour organizers who resurrected our tour of France. Joe is the only man on the trip, and the women adore him. I wish I could see Joe through their eyes more often. My view of Joe is an up-close and personal one. Seeing me come out of the shower this morning, Joe tells me he has a nice hard woody. I replied back, "What is this, the Morning Woody report?" We laughed. After twenty years of waking up with Joe, I have finally found a good way to respond to his comments about his male anatomy and its arousing nature. Laughter, it helps — a lot.

After the gifts and breakfast we go into a nearby town and see a short film about the history of the Cathars and the First Crusade. The film depicts the Roman Catholic Church wiping out fellow Christians who refused to pay homage to the Pope or tithe to the church. It's depressing to be reminded of what can be done in the name of religion and God. My spiritual path has me touring Southern France with a group of people who are connected through Don Miguel. The film leaves me troubled by the philosophy that has so recently given me hope and happiness.

I can't help but question Don Miguel's advice in the Four Agreements. How does the pursuit of happiness under these agreements prevent one person from hurting another? What about evil? Can a person be evil, practice evil, and at the same time never go against themselves, take nothing personally, refrain from making assumptions and do their best? Will the practice of these agreements cancel out humanity's historic urge to do evil to itself?

Our fifth day in Southern France is chilly with overcast skies on the morning we visit stunning abbey ruins. The stones are alive with a unique rosy hue. I take too many pictures as I carefully step around the broken courtyard. Our dreaming guide creates a walking ritual outside the renovated chapel. For some reason when it is my turn to circumvent the circle etched in stone, I take off my shoes to walk the earth with bare feet. Joe is quite engrossed in the ceremony and needs help walking afterwards when we are allowed into the chapel. Jane, our hired Southern France tour guide says this is the first time she has been let into the chapel with a tour group. Sitting with Joe in the back pew while he recovers, I have the strangest dream of sitting on God's lap while he tells me everything is all right. Comforted by God's words and warm embrace, I weep with relief and have no time to explore the lovely chapel before we are ushered out by the building's caretakers.

The second site we visit is an ancient worship area carved out of a rocky hillside. We walk through a crevice in the rocks to enter this house of God. The steps are carved out of the stones that form the hill. The lower walls rise out of the rock and are gradually smoothed out to become supporting arches inside.

After silently roaming the immaculately maintained, empty sanctuary, I sit and dream in a little alcove on the lower level. The alcove is bare except for a large wooden medieval chair and a much more modern music stand next to it. Maybe the locals still use this space, although the downstairs is absent any signs of recent use — except for the flowers placed on the stone window sill beside me.

Afterwards, mellow and light, I climb to the balcony overlooking the main service area and listen while Mary sings. Mary read *The Four Agreements* and found out about the France trip from the web site listed in the back of the book. The trip had been canceled at one point. Joe and I already had the airline tickets and were determined to go to France. I asked tour organizer to see if anyone else wanted to go, too. Mary wanted to go. The journey's theme is *Pathway of the Black Madonna*. Mary Magdalene is believed by some to be the Black Madonna. Mary, who is singing now, has the middle name of Magdalene. We have our own Mary Magdalene on this journey. Spontaneously, Mary will sing beautiful notes of longing, joy and sorrow. There are no words, only arias of heartbreaking sound. Mary says she has no conscious control of her voice; the music comes from her heart.

I imagine I am a Medieval Queen, and Mary is singing for my court below. After the concert I poke around and find an ancient stained glass window of Mary Magdalene in a dark corner of the balcony. Our light-hearted fairy tale ends with a lovely blessing ceremony in front of the ancient stone altar.

After lunch we head for Montsegur, the castle where the Roman Catholic Church finally extinguished the Cathars on March 16, 1244. The Cathars had been brutally attacked by the soldiers of Rome for decades. The castle had been under siege for a year when the Cathars surrendered and were granted fifteen days to get their affairs in order. Legend has it that several Cathars escaped with treasure and made their way to Scotland. The remaining prisoners were given a choice: renounce their faith and join the Catholic Church or be burned alive. The next morning all two hundred and five men, women and children walked into the fire together rather than give up their faith.

The weather gets steadily worse as our tour bus winds its way to the parking lot at the base of a small mountain where the ruin sits. Light rain falls, and a heavy mist permeates the air. We decide to hold a ceremony at the bottom of the trail that leads to the castle. It is a short climb to a memorial erected in memory of the slain Cathars. The grass is slick, and I'm glad I bought sneakers the day before; my cowboy boots would have left me sliding in the mud in the rain.

While walking single file up the path, our dreaming guide asks us to think about what we will offer the fire. What would we like to give up that we are holding onto? I am familiar with these instructions, having been to a Toltec fire ceremony before. The ritual is not exclusively Toltec. Our fellowship held a New Year's Eve service in which we were asked to write down something we did not want to bring into the New Year. Then we burned the paper, symbolically leaving whatever we had written behind us.

Walking up the path, a complete isolated sentence comes into my head: "*Be not so attached to this physical life, it is not so important as your integrity.*" I place a small red flower on the base of the monument when we gather around to begin our ceremony. The memorial is approximately five feet tall and sits on a base stone three and half feet high. The top stone is shaped like an old fashioned keyhole. Engraved in stone are the words, *"Aux Cathares, victims du pur amour chretien"* To the Cathars, victims of their pure Christian love.

Others speak of what they would like to leave behind them and offer their prayers to the metaphorical fire represented by the monument before us. After a moment of silence I walk up to the memorial and separate myself slightly from the rest. I feel the need to be clearly heard as I repeat out loud the sentence that came to me as I walked up the path. I remember each word without effort, "Be not so attached to this physical life, it is not so important as your integrity."

I move back to the outer edge of the group where I am more accustomed to being. Even though I did not offer anything to the fire, I believe I have said what was supposed to be said at this moment. I silently ask the universe for help to stay true to my heart, to not allow myself to negotiate, manipulate and rationalize my heart's desire away or take an expedient, more comfortable alternative.

After our memorial fire ceremony, six of us decide to make the steep climb to the castle. The rest of our group agrees to wait for us in the bus.

Thick green foliage conceals the wooded footpath, except for the few steps in front of our feet. We are lost in our thoughts, and no one speaks as we make our way single file up the narrow path. A thick mist hides the castle, and we can't see how far we must go to reach it. The misty fog that separates us lends a mythological symbolism on our journey to the top.

After a twenty-minute climb, the path starts to level off and the dim outline of a stone wall comes into view. Loud ragged sobbing comes from behind the wall. The woman crying sounds as if her anguish is being torn out of her. I pause, not wanting to disturb her. When the sobbing subsides, Joe and I continue forward.

Once inside, we see that Mary was crying. No singing at Montsegur; the pain is still here in these tumbled down halls. But not much is left of the castle walls. What there is of it is shrouded in a gray mist. The walls blend with the mist so well that I can't be sure where the wall ends and the empty mist begins, thus creating a ghostly, surreal mountaintop to explore.

Finding a spot outside the castle wall overlooking the valley below, I picture myself as the scout looking for the crusaders approach. I envision the siege inside these castle walls all those centuries ago. I know I would rather be one of the scouts, watching from the outside rather than be inside, waiting, with no view. As I indulge my imaginative trip back to the twelfth century, I gain clarity about the issue of dying for a cause. Before today I had concluded that a person should save his or her life rather than die for an ideal. Being alive is what is important, I believed. I was uncomfortable with what that represented, uneasy with my own position — but I didn't know why.

Sitting on the rocks of Montsegur, a clearer understanding eases my soul and resonates with what I know to be true but had not yet been able to see clearly. The issue is not dying for a cause; it is about choosing your integrity before your physical life. What is important is that when the time comes, I have the ability to detach from this life and hold onto my integrity so I can evolve. With this personal evolution, I also help the rest of humanity evolve. Integrity is stronger than physical life; integrity transforms and outlasts this life. The use of integrity in this way, sacrificing one's safety and maybe, ultimately, one's physical life, creates a huge ripple in the pond we call history.

We know this is true because of history. I think of all the people who sacrificed for the résistance during WWII. I think of Egypt's leader, Anwar Sadat, when he signed the Camp David Accord, of Gandhi's hunger strike, of Martin Luther King Jr.'s fight for civil rights, and my personal favorite, Harriett Tubman's repeated efforts to bring freedom to fellow slaves, even though she had already achieved her own. I silently honor all the thousands of others who at some moment choose integrity over life. Our myths are filled with them. We call them heroes.

The six who climbed to the castle regroup and hold a spontaneous ceremony in a small glen a hundred yards from the castle. Love, choice and integrity are offered up by each of us in a toast born of the moment. We feel the bond of adventure and transformation as we form a circle to honor what has happened today and what happened on March 16 all those centuries ago. The mist slowly lifts as we make our way down the trail. By the time we reach the bus the castle is in full view. The fog, our hearts, and our spirits are uplifted this afternoon, and the message of the Cathars is forever imprinted on my soul.

The following morning we hit forty-five minutes of traffic and eat our lunch on the bus. We don't get to our destination, Racomador, until three in the afternoon. We are here to see famous ancient cave paintings. While we wait for the cave tour guide, we have a meeting in a lightly wooded grove outside the cave.

Sitting in a circle on large rocks we share our experiences from the day before. Joe had quite an adventure during the ceremony at the Abbey cemetery the day before and is trying to describe it. At first he only says the ceremony was good, but then the women urge him to tell us more.

Joe's account of Abbey d'Alet Les Bains

The dreaming guide found a circle within the stone pavement outside the renovated chapel door a few feet from the beautiful cemetery. The circle was large enough for all eleven to stand on the rim of the circle engraved beneath our feet. The ten women were asked that one by one walk a spiral within the circle and feel their feminine self, the power and beauty of being the mother earth and then to come and touch me and acknowledge the presence of the male counterpart — to realize and accept that these two energies exist.

All of a sudden my desires of blending in with this group, of being just one of eleven on a Quest, of dropping my maleness for two weeks was being stripped of me in a few seconds. When the group was asked to feel Joe's presence as the other force of life, male, in a second, she segregated me from the group.

Second-by-second, minute-by-minute, day-by-day I was fighting nothing on this trip, past beliefs or what is possible and what is not. I quickly dismissed being used as a symbol for the male being and decided that I would create an energy dream from what was going to happen in the next few minutes.

Earlier I had sensed an energy from this town, from the river's edge and from inside the ruins. I could feel the importance of the abbey from hundreds of years ago. I knew I could create this energy dream because I was to receive a piece of energy from the ten women. When they would make their final circle and face me, maybe to hold out their hand to touch me, I would then borrow some of their energy which I knew would advance the power of my current state to a new intensity. It would be like each person throwing more fuel on the fire.

I knew how to dream, but now I was learning how to accept fuel for that dream. I was most grateful for every one who came in front of me for a moment. I would open my eyes a little now and then to add insight into the power I was receiving. To feel the love and energy each one was sharing in that moment.

As one of the women turned towards me, they sent a shockwave into my dream, my body burst into particles, into dust and then into air, into the wind and circled the abbey and the river. I was no longer body, and my mind no longer had many thoughts at once. I was the wind, and I had eyes, and that was it. My eyes saw a vastness, like looking into the sky at night. No beginning and no end.

I saw two other spirits as I whirled around. They had faces of happiness, though not faces of a human kind, as if they were happy to have this visit. They were like me in size but were composed only of particles that gave them a darkened cloud look as if a leaf could fall through them. Looking at them I realized that I had left my body to meet them. Then I realized I was at that moment the same as them — a living energy cloud.

Moments later my energy body stretched towards Karyn's energy body that was still in the circle on the ground. I felt the need to assure her that I was fine, that I'm not currently in my human body but that I was fine. My mind created a face on her energy body, and she smiled back at me as if to say, I know, its fine. I could feel her happiness and love, so I flew back toward the sky, if only for another minute or two.

Now back in my human body I had everyone's energy inside of me, and it was time for me to walk the circle. I was exhausted from my journey, and the women helped guide me around the circle, and as I fell into my final ceremony dream the following words flowed from my mouth.

"I have lived a thousand lives and now you walk this earth for me."

One of the women tells us she heard the same words come out of Joe's mouth. I don't know who or what was speaking through Joe, but I accept that we are not what we think we are. I accept that I need to be open about what is out there, and what is inside, each of us.

After hearing Joe's tale of the day before, the cave paintings are interesting but not exhilarating. Our next stop is almost unbelievable. Someone, centuries ago, hollowed out a rock mountain and built an astounding place of worship. The stone edifice is built into the cliff, overhanging the town of Rocamadour. The outside structure blends so well with the cliff face that some of the walls *are* the mountain.

Stepping into the dim light of the chapel, I see the altar at the opposite end of the sanctuary and become energized by the sight of the Black Madonna. She is like no other we have seen so far. The Statue has a lustrous gray sheen and is unmistakably Egyptian. The Madonna looks exquisitely graceful and royal while holding a small male child on her lap. This Madonna statue represents a different woman from the one portrayed in the Bible. This Goddess, I am certain, was worshipped openly for ages before the Bible gave us its version of Mary, mother of Jesus.

The chapel is cool and comfortable compared to the hot sun outside. Peace descends as I rest in the gaze of the black Egyptian Goddess. I hear someone singing but do not recognize the language. The woman's lyrical voice fills the small chapel with graceful notes of adoration. I do not open my eyes but sit with the familiar tingling of my body and the hair on my scalp lifts off my head with little dashes of static electricity. I assume the Black Madonna inspires others to sing devotions because the woman singing does not sound like our Mary. Maybe we are infecting others with our love and the people around us are breaking out in song. I smile with the idea and open my eyes. I look around the sanctuary, see some of my group and then bring my gaze over to the right of the altar where I hear the music coming from. It *is* our Mary singing! Only the voice is deeper in pitch, and the song is in another language. Mary has never sung with other people around before; all of her previous spontaneous outbreaks were wordless arias.

After we leave our French translator tells us she thinks she heard the words, "Goddess we adore you," and "lamb of God". Mary doesn't know what she sang, as she has no conscious control over her voice once the singing begins. She lets whatever happens, happen. Mary tells us she doesn't know French or German, which are the languages the translator thought she heard. Joe tells us that a band of energy tightly surrounded his head while inside the shrine. The band disappeared when he stepped out for a moment and returned when he re-entered to hear Mary sing.

We meander through the souvenir booths and gift shops and stop for dinner at a delightful open-air restaurant. The restaurant overlooks the valley and is lit with multi-colored balls strung overhead in a criss-crossing pattern that creates a festive canopy. We discover that the large party at a table near to us is also on a Black Madonna tour. There are eleven of them and eleven of us. They are visiting all the same spots as we are, only in reverse. They started in Paris and are ending in Southern France at St. Marie de la Mer while we are ending our trip in

Paris. They are from Australia, the opposite end of the globe. We think of the other eleven people as our mirrors. I like to think Danica, a woman celebrating her birthday, is my mirror. She is full of life and joy, a welcome reflection for me to own.

June 1, 2002

He is sitting in a hotel lobby in Paris, France, with ten women listening closely to what he has been waiting anxiously to say all day. The small sitting area opposite the reception desk is a rather public place for such an intimate subject, but none of the rooms can comfortably accommodate the whole group. The gathering of women lean in closer to hear above the noise of the hotel guests checking in or strolling out onto the Paris streets.

He begins by repeating that he does not know why he has received this message. Nothing like this has ever happened to him before. And even though he received this message, it doesn't mean he agrees with it or understands it. He said it was an awake dream — he was awake but the experience was more like a dream.

After the message was conveyed to him, he remembers discussing it with Don Miguel. Right after talking with Don Miguel he tells us, he wrote the whole thing down. Of course Don Miguel was not physically in the hotel room; he is in California recovering from a massive heart attack. That is why Don Miguel is not with us right now in Paris. He had a heart attack in February, and the trip had been cancelled and then resurrected, but without Don Miguel.

He is very animated at this point, trying to convey to the group that these things don't happen to him. He again explains that he doesn't know why he was chosen to receive this message, but he was, and he feels strongly that he has to share the message with the group today — tomorrow would be too late. That's why he has asked the tour guide to gather us all together now. Still troubled, he seems unable to relay the message. Stuck on the fact that this has happened to him, he begins explaining that he doesn't understand. Several people in the group call out, "What's the message!" At this prompting, he unfolds a few loose-leaf pieces of paper and begins reading what he had written down early this morning.

His voice is steady and clear and easy to hear. He does not hush his tone, even though he is embarking on an unconventional path. Receiving a message by an unseen, unknown being, discussing that message with his spiritual leader who is physically thousands of miles away; feeling compelled to share this message with ten people, eight of whom he only met a week ago, is not an ordinary experience, not for anyone, and certainly not him. Yet there he is, my husband, newly ordained prophet, reciting messages from, who knows? God, Don Miguel or maybe his own unconscious. Who understands these events? And as Joe asks, "Why me?"

This is the message Joe delivered in the Opera Hotel lobby in Paris, France, on June 1, 2002:

> We are all complete as we stand alone. We need nothing else. To be complete means you hold all, good and evil. We all have evil inside of us, just a very little bit.
>
> Who is delivering the message is not that important, Mother Mary, Mary Magdalene, Jesus. The message being held before us and those they carry with them is important.
>
> The chalice is a vessel, a complete life force, a holder of life, which is precious. In death or spirit, spirit is always with us, and the chalice can be transformed into a powerful complete circle.
>
> The circle is complete as shown. It holds everything before you. Good and evil are always present in all of us. A circle is created when opposite humans come together, yin and yang, male and female. This can be very powerful. Together it makes a human energy circle and the reward is a new life.
>
> The Toltecs and many Prophets from around the earth try to teach us to minimize our evil. Don't beat yourself up for it. Know what is important. Only your own agreements are important. Don't get caught up in all the small stuff. Know your agreements — they will make your evil very small, and your evil will not be able to come out. Having an evil thought is normal. Dismiss it and move on. Acting on it will

*cause your evil to grow within. Remember it is only evil if
that is your belief, agreement or rule.*
  *This is only my story. Take a piece of it, or all of it. Take
none of it. It does not matter if five people hear your story,
ten people, one million or ten million. It is only your story.*

I can't believe what I am hearing. What happened this morning?
He said it happened while I was in the shower. What a bizarre
coincidence, I reflect, remembering my ruminations about evil earlier
this week when riding the bus in Southern France. My body reverberates
with his words when I grasp that his message is addressing the issue
that has been plaguing me throughout the trip. A caffeine rush with
focused intensity hits my body as every cell vibrates with awareness.

When he is done reading what he had written down this morning,
Joe makes it clear he does not wish to discuss with the women what he
has just delivered. His part is done; he feels passing on the message is
what he was supposed to do. He did not want to speak for the message
or in any way interpret it. Then he looks directly at Don Miguel's
apprentice and says he does not want to hear anyone else's
interpretations right now either. I can tell by his tone that he will be
upset if the women start asking questions and offer their opinion, so I
tell our companions that maybe we should go our separate ways for the
rest of the night, even though I am jumping out of my skin and am
hoping Joe will tell me more.

Luckily when we get to our first Parisian sidewalk café a few minutes
later, Joe is ready to talk. He shows me the crinkled notes with the
symbols he saw when he was given the message. Drawn on the paper
in Joe's sloppy scrawl is a chalice, the yin-yang symbol and various
circles, one with a cross, the universal female sign. The world becomes
more vivid, sitting on a Paris sidewalk, going over Joe's early morning
visitation. Anything I focus on is sharply defined in contrast to the
background. The surroundings have less substance, while little things
call out for my attention. Like the woman sitting behind us, alone and
having a drink and eating cocktail pretzels. I notice she is not waiting
for anyone, since after a while she gets up and leaves by herself. But
while she is at the café I sense that I know her on some level, that we
were supposed to meet, and she is here to guide and support us in

some way. Silly thought, an unmistakable reaction to her presence. We have stepped into another world, a world where we are able to perceive another dimension of existence. A non-physical dimension, but not a purely emotional one either. Other people Joe and I encounter at the Paris café, the waiters, the fellow with his dog, the young couple drinking coffee, all strangers; yet somehow familiar. Paris herself is new, but not strange to me.

Deliveries from the cosmos aside, this is our first night in Paris. We have reservations for the Lido nightclub, so we dress up and slip into the Paris nightlife. As an extra bonus to this extraordinary day we are toasting my birthday at the club. My birthday is tomorrow, but we are a romantic couple in Paris tonight. We are warned by the concierge to reserve a taxi early, so we do and are charged twice as much as we should have been. I guess a little evil does reside in all of us. But who cares — not us. We are heady with the spiritual drama of the trip, strolling down the Champs d'Elsyee hours before my forty-fourth birthday.

Still giddy from our first night in Paris, we catch a taxi to take us back to our hotel after the show. We settle into the back seat of a cab close to midnight. I glance at the taxi's meter and notice a digital clock right above it. The clock is in military time and illuminates the numbers 23:59, one minute to midnight and my forty-fourth birthday. I look out the front window and watch as a massive stone tower looms larger as the cab approaches the intersection. Our vehicle stops at a red light directly in front of a three thousand year-old Egyptian obelisk. We are momentarily timeless with the ancient obelisk in front of us and the Arc d'Triumph behind us — exactly as the taxi clock rolls to 00:00. All the circles of time I have experienced being alive for forty-four years come to rest in this moment.

While the moment is commonplace, a cab at a red light, a scrolling digital clock — the moment is extraordinary for the two of us. The 00:00 on the taxi's clock reveals itself as a deeply symbolic reminder of a new era with a message of wholeness and hope. Joe's message of the completeness of a circle is brought back to us in an ingenious but extraordinarily ordinary way.

The ancient hieroglyphs of Egypt, directly in front of us, gives significance to the fact that Joe has been referring to me as KaRa the whole trip. KaRa is my self-given spiritual name, a combination of Ka, the Egyptian word for the vital force of life, and Ra, the Egyptian sun god. Looking at the giant Egyptian obelisk as the clock rolls to 00:00, while I begin my forty-fifth year of life, takes on a grand, synchronistic meaning. We shout, "Happy Birthday, KaRa!" through the open cab windows. We are beside ourselves with joy. What a journey, what a morning, what a night, what a moment! Life is adventurous no matter what Joe and I are doing.

On the morning of my birthday, the tour guide hands out an information sheet about Notre Dame. The pamphlet explains Notre Dame's history from an alchemist point of view. We take the subway to the centuries old Cathedral. The doors on the Paris subway do not open automatically. When the train slows down I have to open the door to get off. Thrilled, I open the door before the stop and hop out onto the platform while the train is still moving. Reaching our destination on an unusually warm day, the hottest of the trip so far, we gather in front of the cathedral and agree to meet in an hour and a half. The cathedral is massive, heavy and ornate. The engravings above the front door alone could be studied for an hour, but we go inside, anxious to see the famous Notre Dame of Paris.

The immense foyer is dark and filled with tourists. Sunday morning Mass is in session in the central chapel. Someone has roped off the pews to ward off the wandering tourists from disturbing the faithful. The right side of the cathedral is packed tight with noisy, snacking, disrespectful tourists. The mindlessly moving, milling about of bodies makes it difficult to see anything of interest. The ceaseless back and forth movement of tourists makes me claustrophobic, though the ceilings look a hundred feet high.

As we make our way around to the left side of the cathedral, the Catholic Mass ends and organ music fills the air. I pause by a massive column and close my eyes to listen. The music sounds horrid to me. The cathedral is filled with a cacophony of discordant sounds, each competing with the other, a harsh overture escalating to a mad spiraling pitch. A madness personified by organ pipes.

Just as I am about to abandon the music, I hear a beautiful note. A few more follow, then a melody is discernible, clarity arising from chaos. The tune is sweet, flowing and melodic. The sweet notes swirl upward and float high above me, dancing inside the whirling confusion of the harsher music of the original score. The light filled aria only lasts a few minutes, until the original madness overtakes the sweet melody, and I break away. The melody sounded like hope to me in this glowering, heavy space. The hope is too weak to withstand this environment, but maybe the memory of its beauty can be transported elsewhere.

When the organ music ends Joe and I are able to sit in the pews and a new Mass begins. I sit and decide to dream. I have done this in all the sites and ruins so far, and I want to see how this historic space resonates with me. I dream I am a multi-armed goddess whose aura is cleansing the harshness that has visited this place. I feel my goddess body expanding, sending out smoky waves of comfort and calmness throughout the building. I feel a touch on my knee and am abruptly taken out of my dream. Goddess interrupted. Annoyed, I see Joe motion to me to rise for a portion of the Mass. He whispers, "I didn't want you sitting while everyone else is standing. It would look disrespectful." Bliss interrupted by a priest: Goddess worship usurped by the Church; like life — like dream.

Soon after, we decide to leave. On the way out I am hit with a combination of thought, feeling and image. The impression made upon my mind is expressed, "This era is over; the power here is waning." We go out the same way we came in, and I look up at the engraved archways above massive wooden doors.

Rows of men sit in judgment of the people standing in line waiting to be weighed worthy of heaven or hell. The entrance of the cathedral permeates with a heavy conviction of guilt, revealing a terrifying place and time to live.

"Good riddance," I mutter as I turn my back to look out over the open courtyard in front of the cathedral. I don't want to wait in the shadow of that message of judgment. I walk about fifty feet away and sit at the feet of a statue.

The monument is a powerful medieval male warrior on top of a warhorse. The statue looks neglected; it is covered in bird shit and shows advanced stages of wear and tear. There is no picture taking, only people cooling off in the bit of shade the spot provides. People sit along its base, oblivious to the identity of the person being honored. I rise and walk to the front of the monument to see the nameplate. The Warrior King is Charlemagne, and I think how appropriate an image this statue is to cap my illumination. His era is over, honored and feared no more.

I catch up with the rest of the gang who have moved on now, and we walk the surrounding streets looking for a place to eat my Birthday lunch. On a street two blocks outside of Notre Dame, I spy an Egyptian statue in a shop window. After lunch, I back-track with Joe and purchase my birthday present; a golden statue of an Egyptian man and women sitting in the dreaming position. They each have one arm around the other. It was the only Egyptian object in the shop, and now — it is mine.

The next site we visit is the Chapel of Immaculate Medals. This place of worship is completely different. Calm and quiet inside, visitors sit peacefully in the pews, either praying or looking silently about them. The haven is emphatically feminine in structure and atmosphere. The sanctuary is filled with circles and globes. Golden balls top every cross. Glass orbs hang from the descending archways on the ceiling. A statue of Mary stands on a globe, while silver threads come from her arms to anchor her to the earth beneath her feet.

Joe's message is mirrored wherever I look. The focal point of the main chapel is an illuminated sphere with lines of energy emanating from its core. I observe the obvious respect the faithful and the tourists alike give the space. The contrast to Notre Dame is unmistakable: one magnificent in architecture, size and history but waning in significance and influence. The other, a place of refuge and healing, welcoming and whole.

The following morning I sit up in bed and squint my eyes to blunt the glare of the overhead light. "What are you doing?" I ask Joe once I see him frantically scribbling on a piece of paper; he is sitting on the floor at the end of Paris hotel room bed.

"I can't talk now; I have to write this down!" Joe huffs back at me.

He is quite tense, and I decide not to push any further and get up and use the bathroom instead. He is done when I come out, and he looks concerned. He wants to know what I think after he shows me what he has written. Another message he tells me, looking to me for an answer to these bizarre episodes. I can't help him and tell him so. "Call Gloria in a little bit," I offer. "She will be up in an hour or two. Ask her. She's been doing this work a lot longer than us. Maybe she can help you."

We met Gloria for the first time on this trip, and Joe has formed a humorous, affectionate bond with her. She is older than either of us and quite beautiful. She has an air of sophistication and worldliness about her. Gloria has shared some outrageous stories with us but has a rather conservative, normal background: mother of three, housewife in New Jersey, successful businessman ex-husband. I hope she can help Joe. I'm not sure what to make of these messages and don't want to influence Joe's experience in any way. I know what they mean to me; they appear to be an answer to my questions about evil and freedom.

When we walked the planet earth together we stepped on some energy. An energy delivered a message to my human body. Why it picked my human body and not an elder Dreamer I can only guess. Maybe it recognized my spirit, I don't know if a male spirit mattered. Maybe it was open at the right time. Once the message hit my human body it is possible it got confused and the message corrupted. Humans cannot deliver a perfect message. Spirit energy can deliver a message to a spirit energy, at the third attention, a more pure conversational level.

There is more, but it sounds like a conversation Joe is having with himself, rather then a message like before. This second message is almost a disclaimer. Poor guy, he really looks a bit freaked out. I hope Gloria gets up soon.

In the afternoon our translator teaches us how to say the French name correctly, *Char* rhymes with *jar* and *tres* sounds like the beginning of the word *truck*, Char — tres. Chartres is a cathedral dedicated to Our Lady in a town called Chartres. Approximately one hour from Paris, if you catch the express train, an hour and forty-five, if you are unlucky enough to take the local. The cathedral reminds me of a castle that Harry Potter and his sorcerer friends might live in. Set up on a hill, overlooking the town, I imagine witches and warlocks flying on broomsticks through the vast spaces between the open buttresses at night while the townspeople sleep unknowingly in their beds.

We have already wasted three hours today, waiting for everyone to gather, missing trains because of poor planning and silly distractions. Now aggravated with my traveling companions, I wait at the entrance while we are asked to meditate on who we really are while we tour the site. We are urged to ask ourselves who is behind the mask we wear for the outside world.

I try to shake off the negative feelings I have let build up before I enter the cathedral. As I enter I decide I will no longer follow but explore the cathedral on my own and leave the group to wander on its own. I make a beeline for the far left wall where there is a warm glow of candles. The area is designated for Madonna and child worship. I sit down to meditate and become more relaxed and open to the beauty of my surroundings.

Leaving the Madonna, I wander aimlessly, exploring the nooks and crannies I inadvertently run into. Just as Notre Dame in Paris was a sacred gathering place before it was Christian, Chartres also has pre-Christian roots. Druids worshipped here and an even more ancient people before that. The signs of the Zodiac are embedded in brilliant colored glass. Looking at the unfamiliar pictures in Chartres' stain glass windows, I wonder what unusual religious leader allowed such esoteric symbols to be displayed so prominently in a Catholic Church.

Next I wander into a chapel behind the main service area. Chartres is so immense four or five services could be held at once. The chapel is dominated by an enormous statue of a woman with her hands uplifted toward heaven with three supporting angels surrounding her. The magnificent stone woman before me is clearly in heavenly ecstasy. Unusual for such a large statue to depict a devout woman; all the other sanctuaries I visited had a male figure reaching up to God or heaven. The women were usually holding a child or looking up at Christ while kneeling at his feet.

I sit before her, wanting to worship in this most unique chapel. I express my gratitude in prayer for finding a religious setting where my gender is represented and revered. It means so much to feel included in the sacred bliss that religions hold out for us to reach for. Seeing that someone created this representation of the feminine receiving fully the gift of heavenly love, by herself, not in a supporting role, is glorious.

Dreaming in one of the wooden chairs in front of the statue I acknowledge my desire to write a book. But what am I to say in this book? I worry about what happened with all the major religions, beautiful loving words turned inside out and used to support centuries of war. The massacres of human life, innocent people and children slaughtered in the name of God, someone else's God. How can any message be helpful when it can be corrupted so easily?

Feeling distressed, I ask for help in my dream. I ask for help from Rita, my spiritual guide and friend, Rita, who taught Joe and I how to dream. A moment after seeking Rita's help, the idea of integrity comes to mind and the message I relayed at Montsegur comes to me again. "Do not be so concerned with this physical life, it is not so important as your integrity." The reminder is followed by, "*I already gave you the message at Montsegur.*"

At that moment the lights flare on, as if the light in my head is in sync with the cathedral. Literally enlightened, I linger on in a comforting dream state. Unfortunately the euphoria doesn't last long, and I am troubled again, now with the question of how does one define integrity.

I imagine many German citizens thought they were acting with integrity when they followed Nazi orders and committed atrocious, vile acts against humanity. Can't integrity be distorted too?

An image of a chalice comes to me. A chalice was in Joe's first message. A chalice is the symbol of my new fellowship, Unitarian Universalism. I consider the seven guiding principles of the Unitarian Universalist's faith. The first one I know by heart: *the inherent worth and dignity of every person.*

I asked for help, and what better help than the culmination of teachings that have evolved into an open loving faith? The seven principles summarize the essence of what Unitarian Universalists promote in the world religion arena. The seven guiding principles are the main reason I joined the UU congregation near my home. Maybe integrity can be defined, with the help of evolving guidelines that draws from the best humanity has to offer.

What a boon to know there are words that cannot easily be corrupted by one group to use against another. What an amazing place to receive such gracious messages of hope.

As I come out of my deep meditative state, Mary's voice fills the cathedral as it resounds brilliantly off the marble columns. The miracle of humanity's ecstasy for worship is manifested in Mary's voice. Hearing the poignant sound while sitting in front of a striking work of art celebrating the feminine love of God is wondrous. I am overwhelmed with gratitude for being exactly where and who I am.

Joe and I decided to visit the temple on our free day in Paris, since we had walked past the square so many times on our way to the subway station. To go almost anywhere from our hotel we had this beautiful temple dedicated to Magdalene in our sight. The temple is as large as a small city block, but no one else thought to visit it — until we told them what we had found.

Sometimes what we are looking for is as large as day and just as obvious. I see the lesson of not overlooking what is right before my eyes. I learn from a pamphlet given out by a curator that the building is used for concerts, World Youth Day gatherings and Jubilee celebrations. The structure was inaugurated as the Square of Hope in 1999. What a wonderful way of using a house of God, a feminine house of God.

The exterior perimeter is decorated with large Corinthian style columns; the building is more a Greek temple than a church. The inside is open, airy and conspicuously void of crosses. The main sanctuary houses a large statue of a pregnant Mary Magdalene in a basket held by three angels.

We have spent eleven days looking at Black Madonnas, searching for clues to the real relationship between Jesus and Mary Magdalene, and right here a block and a half from our hotel is a statue of a pregnant Mary Magdalene.

The usual organ music is playing as we explore the outer rim of the large airy sanctuary. When I sit down in a pew to meditate, a young Asian woman comes in, sets up a music stand near the pulpit and begins playing her violin. Delicate notes float out over the pews and wind around the hard marble walls. What a contrast to the horrible discordant mad organ music at Notre Dame a few days earlier.

We take in a view of Paris as we exit from the grand set of stairs the Temple is set upon. On either side is the Egyptian Obelisk and Arc d'Triumph in direct line with the Temple. The hairs on the back of my neck stand up as I am reminded of my birthday adventure in the cab. Joe and I gaze out, amazed, and laugh at how our lives also seem to be lining up with a meaning, as yet, unknown.

Our final day in France, I wake up with enough time to have the last breakfast included with my hotel stay. I enter the dining room and stop. I don't remember this room. I look for a familiar face and see only strangers nibbling croissants and sipping coffee. I turn around and go down the hall. Maybe there are two dining rooms, and I always go to the other one. I circle around the floor but don't find any other place to eat. Perhaps I am on the wrong floor. I wait for the elevator and go up a flight and then down to the lobby. No, there is no other floor with a dining room.

I return to where breakfast is being served and wonder how the room could look so unfamiliar. I walk over to the coffee station and pour myself a cup of strong Parisian coffee. As I move towards an empty table someone from my group comes in and I am relieved to know that I didn't accidentally stumble into the twilight zone. The aura of magic has lifted. I'm back on earth again, although I know I never really left. Whatever has changed has changed in me. That is all that ever really does.

Gathered here in the mystery

Joe and I wake up to a spectacular sunrise in the meditation tower at The Oaks. The room we were supposed to sleep in was occupied. The college student sleeping in our usual bed refused to give up the room just because the manager at the Oaks goofed and double booked the center. We lucked out and were able to sleep in a meditation tower built on the edge of the Long Island Sound.

The tower has floor-to-ceiling windows on three sides. The sunrise over the water is breathtaking, and we are grateful we can greet the day in such a magnificent manner. But I am still sleepy and try to go back to sleep after the sun climbs into a less dramatic position in the sky.

As I drift off to sleep, I catch myself inventing an entirely different reality that is to become my dream. I am able to stay aware of my thoughts as I drift off into that imaginary realm, where what is solid and concrete while awake, now gives way to the fantastical whimsy of dream.

I catch myself on the cusp of being awake and being in a dream, and I wonder if what I think is reality is really another creation as well. Maybe the associations I create in my mind while awake are so strong and so deep that I can only conceive of 'reality' as I have always perceived the world to be. To our mind, our dreams are as valid when we are asleep as 'reality' is when we are awake. How do we know what is real?

During our third Mitote ceremony later that night Joe is asked to call in the Sun and me the Moon. I try to listen to the people who speak before me, but I'm distracted; I want to think about what I will say. I tell myself not to make a big deal and to speak from my heart. This advice sounds rather corny when I say the words to myself, but I manage to let go of the effort:

"I call upon the power and image of the moon. Just as it waxes and wanes so do our lives. Whether it is a half moon or crescent moon we see, the moon is always full, a round circle, complete and perfect, just as we are."

When asked to release the moon after our all night ceremony, I feel the words come forth again and say:

"I release the moon so we may enjoy its beauty and to remind us that what we perceive is not always what is. We may perceive ourselves as only half full or almost empty but in essence we are full, round and complete. It is just the reflection of ourselves that has been obscured by the distortion of light."

Joe's message in France is the inspiration, but the words feel like they have been whispered into my heart, then exit my lips.

July 2002

Sometime before leaving for my writing workshop, a client asks me if there is any particular book I would like from the book warehouse she is visiting. I tell her I'd like anything by His Holiness the Dalai Lama. She brings me *The Art of Happiness*. I am somewhat surprised by the title. Happiness seems too base a pursuit for such a lofty person as the Dalai Lama.

What is happiness?

I'd read Buddhist books, Toltec books, New Age and even psychic books. I went to a conference called *The Heart of Happiness*. The speakers and authors gave their version of what brings us to happiness. They spoke of desire, the heart's desire, doing what you love, being grateful for what you have and accepting what is. All of which rings true, but doesn't clarify for me why so many people in this day and age, and especially in this country, who seem to have more of everything still appear unhappy.

Why are there so many anti-depression and anti-anxiety commercials on TV? Why all the worrying and nervousness? Why is complaining the glue of so many conversations? A quote from His Holiness the Dalai Lama helps me decipher the paradox of lack of happiness in the midst of plenty:

"Sometimes people confuse happiness with pleasure."[1]

The simple statement explains why so many activities that bring pleasure — shopping, eating, drinking, sex, gifts, and electronic gadgets — don't bring lasting happiness. Pleasure and happiness are two different animals. In the United States, the popular culture worships at the altar of pleasure. Magazines, TV, movies, billboards and the market economy are dependent on relaying the message — pleasure equals happiness.

I find I am most happy when I'm grateful. It doesn't matter whether I'm grateful for a peach or a flower or my sons or my husband or my home; when I'm feeling grateful, I'm happy.

When I purchase something new, it is a pleasure, and I feel happy for the moment, maybe even for the whole day. But I can't constantly buy things to create this temporary happiness for practical reasons — not enough money and for psychological reasons — the law of diminishing returns will at some point set in. However, I can try and cultivate an attitude of gratitude that stays with me all the time. That would bring happiness full-time.

Grateful to be able to take a week for myself, I arrive at Omega under sunny skies and take pleasure in navigating the country roads I traveled a year ago. After checking in and unpacking in the little dorm room that reminds me of a monk's quarters, I head for the Sanctuary. There is no meditation class scheduled, but I feel compelled to go and say hello to the space.

A lightly wooded forest surrounds the path leading to the Sanctuary, which is situated on top of a hill. Berry bushes, ferns and other wild greenery line the footpath. While none of forest undergrowth has been planted on purpose, the foliage manages to create a mosaic of green tranquility, almost a foreshadowing of the potential calm waiting at the end of the walk.

I approach the Sanctuary, a wooden building with an open pyramid-shaped roof. The first portico is open on both ends with shelves and a bench to store shoes and other unneeded paraphernalia.

I walk barefoot along the wood deck that creates a path through the Koi pond. I can see the water lilies and golden fish in the water. I look closer to see if I can spot any frogs. I continue walking along the wood deck on the outside of the building to get to the only door in the main structure. Breathing deeply, beginning my first five-day retreat on my own, I open the door and let myself in.

The room is an amazing space. The wave rock wall that spans two of the four walls is my favorite feature. The slate wall looks alive. The curve at the top of the rock wall gives the impression of motion. The square gray rocks that have been so carefully placed underneath the wall sculpture express earth and grounded-ness. An open thirty-foot pyramid shaped ceiling offsets the rock walls' solidity with an open, airy, boundless atmosphere. The room is empty of furniture except for meditation pillows and backjacks. I settle down and breathe in the air while the stillness of the space encircles me. A feeling of contentment seeps into my bones. Sighing, I mutter just loud enough for the rocks to hear, "Oh, how I love this place."

Monday, the next morning at seven a.m., I return to the Sanctuary for the first meditation class of the week. The teacher's name is Gayle. She reminds me of someone's Aunt Clara. No ghoulish sunken eyes like the last meditation teacher I sat with in the Sanctuary last summer. That teacher looked like the living dead, deathly pale with dark circles under her eyes, bone thin and anemic looking. Last year's teacher told us how she was on a sabbatical so she could meditate more. After looking at her I had decided too much meditation can definitely be a bad thing. Gayle, on the other hand, looks plump and healthy. No hushed, well-modulated tones emit from Gayle. She speaks in a conversational manner with a pleasant southern accent. She rings her Tibetan bells and for twenty minutes guides us to drop our thoughts and be present.

After meditation and breakfast, I make my way to the Lake house — the same building I was in a year ago for the Four Agreements workshop with Don Miguel and Rita. Lynda Barry is as funny as I remember, maybe funnier. She reads a Rumi poem to help us understand the magic involved bringing stories to life on paper. I'm not sure I understand the poem or the connection, but the aura the poem evokes lingers well into the morning.

Car, again, is the first noun Lynda selects, and we write a memory about a car we have known. All the cars in my past parade before me, and I pick the Chevy Road Runner my father bought after the divorce to write about. I was learning how to drive at that time, and the car was way too much muscle for me, but he let me drive even though I could barely reach the accelerator. When the stories are read out loud, I am impressed with the other students in the class.

Lynda never critiques when someone shares his or her writing. Instead she kneels close to the reader as they overcome their initial shyness of sharing out loud. Sometimes the class is in tears as it listens to the poignant memories put to paper.

The next morning the walk through the forest is supernatural with the mist rising in ghostly swirls off the dense moist flora. Tiny drops of moisture cling to every leaf and glisten in the dappled sunlight that illuminates the wooded path. I feel a little spooked walking by myself in the fog, not really sure why I am so compelled to get up early and make my way to the Sanctuary yet again. As I walk through the enchanted forest, I can't help but think of Don Miguel and wonder what he has gotten me into. It was his workshop that cemented my embarking on a spiritual journey. I pick out an inconspicuous spot to meditate and wait for the formal sitting to begin.

Before ringing the bells the meditation teacher asks everyone to take a moment to honor the sacred space that the Sanctuary holds. To recognize the multitude of spiritual masters who have shared this same space, to be aware of the consciousness that still permeates the building itself. She then asks us to look at the other people sharing this morning's meditation. I look at the people sitting to the side and in front of me, then turn around to see if anyone is behind me.

My eyes meet the eyes of a woman sitting behind and a little to the left. Our eyes meet, and I fall in love. I fall in love with this woman I have never seen before. I have no desire to know her, not even her name; I only know I love her. Love her as another human being. And in that brief meeting the love expands to include all of humanity. We are bound as the air becomes electrically charged with the creation of an energetic channel linking this unknown, lovely woman and me.

That evening I return to the Sanctuary. The teacher seems to know when my mind is wandering. Her gentle voice will pull my attention back to my breath so that whatever thoughts have roped my attention can be gently dropped. She is speaking about the fourth level of awareness, a level of clarity accompanied by a sense of bliss. I am reminded of a lesson from the Wisdom Group about clearing the pipes of communication. The more pure the channel of communication is, the easier the message can be received with love and pure intent. Since meditation had gone so well this morning I decide to send a message to Joe at home. Let me open a channel of love to my honey. Why not play a little while I sit here in this phenomenal space? The Tibetan bells ring out and I sink immediately into a familiar focused meditative state.

I sing-song Joe's name. Joooeeeey. No one else calls him that but me. I call out Joey, Joooeeey in my mind. As the last eeee sound of the third Joey leaves my mind to join the soft evening air, I feel a wave of fast moving energy. A huge swirling eyeball with a giant smoking genie tail spins out of nowhere and flies straight at me.

The giant blue eye stops abruptly in front of me. "Yeah, what do you want?" demands the eyeball, while hovering inches from my face in a spot directly between my eyes.

There are no words or sounds heard by my ears. But the message — Yeah, what do you want? — is as clear as a bell. The message relays an attitude that I had somehow disrupted the eyeball from doing whatever it had been doing prior to the eye answering my call. Before I can reply to the question, the eyeball looks quickly to the left and to the right.

With less intensity, but with the same clarity and attitude, the eye asks, "What are you doing?"

"Nothing, nothing," I reply with my mind, leaning back to be as far away from the inquiring eye as possible. Now I'm scared. What did I conjure? I stare nervously at the big blue eyeball. Joe has big blue eyes. The swirling eyeball is somehow like Joe, but not my human Joe, maybe a wind Joe or an unexplainable ancient energy Joe. My body is frozen with electric energy that keeps me from getting up or moving. Freaking out but totally engaged, I don't want to end whatever is going on. But as suddenly as the eye appeared, it disappears.

I keep my eyes closed and take deeper breaths. As my breathing becomes steadier, I feel as though — from the waist up — I am stretched towards the ceiling. My upper body is full of buzzing light and is pulling up, up, upwards. My elastic vibrating body then forms a pyramid with my head as the capstone at the top.

Unfurled and transparent, I contemplate the essence of a clear channel and the clarity the teacher spoke of earlier. Transported by an unknown force, I am in love again. Surrounded by love, with no object to love. Expanding, buzzing, dissolving in love.

After dinner I make my way through the woods, following the sign that points to the Shamanic Healing tent. Thirty feet into the forest, I see the tent through the twilight mist that has descended between the trees. The tent could have been bought at K-Mart and does not look exceptional but for the few Native American articles placed near the doorway. I'm not sure what will be inside of the tent. I'm not even sure why I booked the session. Something different, I concluded; something different, yes. I was looking for something different. I didn't know when I signed up on Sunday night that I would already have experienced an abundance of unexplainable encounters before my Tuesday evening appointment.

Too late to cancel. I make my way to the opening and poke my head inside. A blond woman in stretch pants and a cotton shirt motions me inside. She looks like someone I could bump into at a PTA meeting. I feel slightly cheated that a more indigenous looking person isn't the Shaman.

The blond woman tells me her name is Gail. Another Gayle I note to myself. I have met three Gayles, two at Omega and one at the Wisdom Group. This Gail is also from Connecticut. She has had Native American and Celtic teachers. She is part of a Shamanic group but came into Shamanism on her own. She has heard of Don Miguel, and we agree that Dreaming is much like what she calls Journeying.

When she asks me why I am here tonight I tell her honestly that it is mostly out of curiosity. Then I tell her about the eyeball. A Shaman is probably a good person to tell; maybe she can explain what happened somehow. After hearing my adventure, Gail asks if I have a power animal. I tell her no, I do not. She tells me I need a Sacred Space protector, which is similar to a totem, but with a more specific purpose. She believes that I am in need of spiritual protection.

That unsettles me a bit, and I agree to journey with her to find my Sacred Space Protector. She could retrieve the protection for me, but tells me I have good energy and will be able to find one while she drums.

Gail shows me where to lie down, face up on a blanket laid out in the middle of the tent. She asks me to visualize a cave, if possible a cave I have entered once upon a time. "Approach the cave and go inside, there will be animals there," she explains. "The one who is your power animal will make itself known three times; that is how you will know it is the right one."

I visualize a cave I saw in southern France from the tour bus window. The opening was situated in the woods alongside the winding country road that spiraled around a small mountain. I approach the cave as instructed and go inside. I feel the impostor when Gail's drumming continues, but nothing happens to me while in the cave. Maybe I need to visualize more details; I conjure up a wolf then a deer. The more animals I visualize, the easier the journeying becomes.

A slow parade of animals flits across my mind's eye, but none of them resonate with me or show up more than once. I was hoping a horse would be my power animal, since a horse convinced me to go to the *Spirit in Business* convention. But the horse in my mind's eye walks on by; it is followed by a line of equally disinterested animals.

Feeling stupid lying here, I wonder if I should stop wasting Gail's time and drumming when all of a sudden — BAM! — a bird with huge eyes pops right in front of my face. The same way the eyeball appeared earlier only closer to my face. But this time I don't see it approach. The bird is just there. Maybe it is an owl; the eyes are so large compared to the rest of its face.

In what seems to be a response to my thought, the bird moves back a few inches from my face, and I see I am mistaken. The bird is a hawk with dark coloring around the eyes that gives it the appearance of an owl at such close range. Now I can see the hooked beak and smooth dark feathers around the eyes. I can't see anything else; the bird is still so close to my face. A white peacock, a bird that showed up in my backyard one day, comes into focus next.

I had almost forgotten about that bizarre morning when I looked out my back window and saw an albino peacock walking around my backyard! I took a picture. I didn't think anyone would believe me if I told them a rare tropical bird had landed in my yard. When I stepped out on the back deck to snap the picture, the bird flew, then perched on the garage roof. The exotic bird stood still — posing for pictures, fanning its long white feathers out and over the roof tiles. When I let the dog out before I left the house that morning, the graceful white bird flew to my neighbor's yard and that was the last I saw of it.

I intuit that the bird in my face is letting me know its feathers are white. I count that as the second appearance and ask the vision for the third and final occurrence that will clinch a successful journey. With that request I am flying over the forest, looking down through the trees and watching the ground whiz by. I am not riding the bird; *I* am the bird, powerfully flying over the trees. The perspective from the air leaves me breathless.

The scope of my vision is enlarged to encompass acres of land below and beyond me. My exhilaration ends when I spot a rabbit zigzagging on the forest floor, and I begin to descend as if giving chase. That is enough proof for me, and I focus on the drumming that had receded from my attention when the hawk appeared.

I wiggle my toes and slowly open my eyes.

"That was quite a journey," Gail says as she puts aside her drum. She then asks me to tell her exactly what happened.

I tell her how there was no doubting the intent of the bird that appeared from nowhere. How at first I had to visualize the animals, but the hawk was different. The hawk's sudden, unimagined appearance is exactly like other awake dreams I have had recently. The dream starts with my imagination then takes off with a life of its own.

Gail explains that, Shamanically speaking, a bird of prey is associated with visionaries and messengers. A hawk has wide vision, but at the same time, is focused. She tells me my focus may make some people uncomfortable.

The following morning Lynda has us writing from another person's point of view. She instructs the class to use what we have recently written and rewrite the piece from another character's perspective. Writing from someone else's point of view is more difficult. I guess that is what makes a great fiction writer great; the ability to get into someone else's skin. The memory I am told to rewrite is a dark one.

I am crouched down and bent over because I cannot stand
all the way up. The air is musty and closed in. The space is
dark, except for some light coming in from the small basement

window on the right side of the room. Not a room really, a crawl space. There are cobwebs in the corners and dead flies on the ground. The floor beams overhead squeak when someone walks above our heads. That is what we are waiting for — the squeaking to stop. That's when we know Mom has left the house, and it is safe to come out. There is a cleaned up area against the wall nearest to the entrance. That is where my brother Brian sits waiting. I don't know why I agreed to skip school with him today; school isn't that bad, not bad enough to sit down here for hours.

Who knows when Mom will leave?

I hope it is soon; it is so boring down here. I look over at Brian and see he is settling in. I can't believe he actually sat here all day once. Mom never went out, and he had to stay in the crawlspace until he was supposed to come home from school. That would have been six or seven hours. He must really hate school to do that.

I don't hate school, but today I am drained; I'm tired and my head hurts. I don't want to try to look regular today — and that is why I agreed to skip school. I'm too tired to pretend I'm like the other kids. But this, I think, is worse. I don't feel any better down here; I feel sick, as if hiding for real is sicker then hiding in plain sight. I'm used to hiding at school. I am so sorry I decided to do this. Brian has a way of talking me into these things, and I do them even when I don't want to. Listening to the noises upstairs, I almost feel like I am dead and buried. I'm dead and quiet and not moving, while the lucky alive people are upstairs, and they don't even know I'm dead.

I think Spurs the cat must have killed a mouse or something and dragged it down here. It doesn't smell right, and I can't see into the corners. There is no way I am going to go look either. I remember when we found Marlboro down here, stiff as a board. God that was gross. Who knows what might be down here?

Brian is sitting there like it is nothing. Like this isn't the most disgusting place in our house. He almost looks comfortable. I guess that is how he managed to stay here all day one day. I don't know how he gets me to do these things. I guess I do it, because I know how lonely he is. I know we are all that he has. I always feel so sorry for him that I can't say no. He is so smart, so good at school, top of his class every year, and yet he gets no joy from learning anymore.

Mom said they wanted him to go to that genius school, but he was too afraid to go; he would have had to live away from home. I wish things were different; I really don't want to be here with him.

I try to write the piece from my brother Brian's point of view but quickly get depressed. What must it have been like to be in Brian's skin back when we were kids? He was three years older than me and was my source of information on all manner of adult subjects — money, politics, procreation and religion. Painfully shy, geeky, brilliant and lonely, very lonely as a teenager. Not a single male friend I can remember. When he was younger he could get away with hanging out with girls. His gentle, sensitive nature fit right in for the most part. But once adolescence starts, a girl is a girlfriend, not just a friend, and Brian didn't swing that way.

Nobody knew it back then, we suspected, but no one knew for sure that Brian was gay, perhaps not even Brian. But that ended up being the least of Brian's problems. And being gay in high school is a problem. Being different in high school is a problem. And Brian would rather sit in the crawl space under our house all day and skip school than face the tyranny that is teenage conformity. He wasn't the type that got beaten up; he was the kind that disappeared. Nobody missed him when he wasn't there — they didn't notice him when he was.

I finish writing when Lynda tells us to put down our pens. I didn't enjoy that memory at all. I won't use Brian again. I've tried crawling inside his head before, when I was begging him to take his meds when he lived in a basement apartment that Joe and I built for him in our first house. It isn't a pretty place to be, inside a schizophrenic's head.

I admire Wally Lamb's ability to create the character in *She's Come Undone*. How he described her descent into madness. How he became her, to tell the story in such a convincing and tender way. I don't want to imagine Brian's gentle soul being pulled down into a never-ending chaotic nightmare. No, I won't use Brian as a character anymore, too heartbreaking. So heartbreaking, I stopped believing in God for a long time. I couldn't find any love or justification in my brother's suffering. There is no justification; no one deserves that kind of suffering; no karma can explain it. It just is. Brian just is.

Reviewing my brother's life reminds me of a story a worship leader at my fellowship retold during a service one day. A mentally retarded boy is on a walk with his father. They walk past a baseball field where the neighborhood kids are playing ball. The father is sad because his son cannot play like the other children. Today his son is not content to walk by. His son wants to play. The father is anxious because he knows his son is not capable of playing baseball. But the other children see that the boy wants to join in, and they invite him over. They make sure he has a chance at bat, they pitch him a soft, hittable lob, and they show him how to run around the bases. They let him play until he is tired and asks to stop.

The father's gratitude towards the 'normal' children leads him to believe that what is important in life is not his son's disability, but our human reaction to someone's inability to be like us. How we react and accept or not accept those who cannot be what most of us are — sane, straight, mentally competent, and physically able.

I decide to ask Lynda during the break whether her method of writing will work if the events being written about are real and not fiction. Lynda asks me for an example, which takes me aback; now I have to relay a story when I was expecting a quick answer. I tell Lynda the swirling eyeball meditation story. The fantastic encounter is still fresh in my mind. Lynda listens attentively and after I tell her what happened to me on Tuesday, I make sure she knows that I am a 'soccer mom' and drive a mini-van in case she thinks I come from a California commune where swirling eyeballs visit often. I'm not as weird as I sound, I explain.

Lynda replies with "Look who you're talking to."

Lynda is weird. Weird in an attractive way, in a way that makes you hope some of the weirdness will rub off on you. That's because Lynda is funny, really funny, warm and smart. "Describe meditation" Lynda requests.

I am somewhat suspicious. Aren't we having this writing class at Omega, a holistic learning campus? How can she not know how to meditate? I start by explaining the basics, breathing, watching thoughts, stilling the mind. I tell her about Gayle and last year's meditation teacher. I tell her that concentrating on breath alone bores me so what I do at home is more helpful to me. If, for instance, I have a problem at work, when I meditate I put the problem in the form of a question, and I throw it out to the universe with no expectations. Then I sit back, breath and wait.

The key, I go on to explain, is no expectations. I may not get an answer, but I have found that most often something will eventually come up. I motion from the back and base of my skull up to the top of my head. I get out of my own way by releasing any expectations or preconceived notions of what the answer is. I don't spin my wheels. Somehow the best thing to do will make itself known to me when I let go.

"I can see the whole thing, the eye episode, the meditation teacher, all of it. Write that way, just like you told me." Lynda says, after listening intently.

Now I know why she wanted me to tell a story and explain meditation. To illustrate that writing is good story telling.

"And the problem solving with meditation, that's good. I'm going to write that down," Lynda discloses, ending our conversation.

By Friday morning, the last morning of my week at Omega, my ability to perceive the other people meditating in the Sanctuary is pronounced. I cannot tell which consciousness energy field belongs to which person, but I can feel when someone joins in. I know I perceive the situation accurately because today, after we had been meditating with eyes closed for about ten minutes, I heard someone come in and sit down. A few moments later I felt a new vibration in the room. Not a sound vibration, but a sensation in my mind's energy field. When the meditation is over, and I open my eyes I see a woman I have become friendly with this week is the person who joined the group late. Like me, she is a regular attendee of the morning meditation classes this week.

While I've never seen energy fields, I can feel from which direction they are coming in relation to me. The same morning I feel the new energy join in I also become aware of an energy field that exudes a vibration of clarity that differs from the rest of the energy in the room.

I imagine a clear blue pool of shallow water in my mind's eye when I first sense the unfamiliar consciousness of this new person. When the meditation is over I look in the direction of the energy and notice a middle-aged Asian American woman I had not seen in the group before this morning. She is alone, over by the windows, and is still meditating. When I ask the meditation teacher later at breakfast, she confirms that the woman was indeed the new, clear energy source at our sitting.

I know the energy I have been encountering this week is not a part of me. But the images that come to me, to aid me in conceptualizing the quality of energy, are of my own making. The imaging is unprompted, and I presume they arise from associations of whatever I deem is clear and calm, exciting or threatening. A swirling genie eyeball image spontaneously emerges when the energy is threatening and sudden. A clear blue pond comes to mind when the energy is crystalline and calm. I imagine the image is there to help me make sense out of the energy I am confronting in that moment. The illustration gives my mind something to hold onto when what is happening has no reference points. No reference points — I have never been aware of experiencing anything like this before.

Lynda is late for our last class, which is highly unusual; she always starts class exactly at nine. She is late, she tells us, because she had to prepare for a special ending for the workshop. This is her third year teaching at Omega. Some students have attended all three years; others two years, and some, like me, only once. She told us earlier in the week that she wrote her bestseller *Cruddy* in long hand with a paintbrush. This morning she cut up part of her original manuscript and put the pieces in envelopes. She gives each student an envelope with a piece of her manuscript inside. Each envelope is marked with only a 1, 2 or 3 and is handed out according to whether you were a three year, two year, or one year student. I open my envelope and look down at my piece of Lynda's manuscript. It has one word written on it in red paint:

Power.

At the end of class I wait in line to get my Angel book signed by Lynda. I could have asked her to sign one of the books she authored, but I want Lynda's words in my journal. Lynda is taking time to speak with each student personally. I know it is going to be awhile before I get

to the head of the line. I remember how long it took Lynda to answer
the one question I asked her yesterday. Finally, my turn, and I walk up
to Lynda.

She looks me straight in the eye and says, "What you said yesterday
stayed with me. I tried that meditation technique, because I didn't know
what to do for class today, so I threw it out there and waited. And the
answer came to me! You should write that eyeball story, start with the
description of the first meditation teacher, and then write about Gayle.
Tell people the story and teach them the meditation thing."

Flabbergasted by what I hear, I am momentarily speechless until I
remember to ask her to sign my journal. The teacher had remembered
what I said! I had helped the teacher! By the time I reach my chair, I am
discounting everything I have just been told. A voice inside my head tells
me, "Lynda is only being encouraging; she does that with all the students."

"But she remembered the eyeball and Gayle's name, I only
mentioned Gayle's name in passing, it must have made an impression
on her," I reply back to the voice in my head. "Lynda's brilliant; she
probably has a photographic memory or something, I'm telling you,
she is a sympathetic writing coach. Get a grip. It's nothing."

I know these thoughts cannot be stopped; but I don't have to listen
to them or follow them as they wind around — a tortured internal conflict
with no resolution. I decide instead to allow myself to feel the happiness
the whole morning has brought to me. Class doesn't officially end until
noon. There is still time to see if I can hear one more of Sister Alice's
gospel songs.

I leave my notebooks and take a short walk to Stillwater. I know
where to go; I had taken Sister Alice's sampler class on Wednesday
afternoon. Lynda was the one who encouraged the class to sample
Sister Alice's gospel class. One of Sister Alice's songs in particular keeps
running through my head this morning. The song is called *We are
Walking in the Light of God*. I liked this song best of the three songs
Sister Alice taught us that afternoon. It was a dream come true to sing
gospel music with a choir, and so much more fun than I ever expected.
Sister Alice's directing talent and encouraging compassion had us
sounding great in an hour and a half.

I am hoping to hear the song one more time, or at the very least,
thank Sister Alice. The tune had come into my head during this morning's

meditation, bringing about such a deliciously loving feeling that I want to thank her.

As I round the corner and Stillwater comes into sight, I see Sister Alice and her brother getting into a van. I figure the last thing she needs is one more person saying thank you — there are fifty people in her class, and she probably has been thanked enough. I turn my attention away from the departing Sister Alice and look over at the people gathered outside to say goodbye. They are arranged for a group photo; a class member is taking the picture. I offer to take the picture for her so she can be in the photo. She takes me up on my offer and a few more classmates hand me their cameras so they can have a group picture also. We turn around and wave to Sister Alice and her brother as they drive up the dirt road that leads them out of Omega.

I raise the camera to my eye and position the shot to get the entire class in. I see through the lens the full choir waiting expectantly for my cue to smile. I lower the camera and say, "But first you have to sing *Walking in the Light of God.*"

Without missing a beat, the class starts singing the chorus I have been hearing in my head all morning. I sing along and pretend to be Sister Alice. As the song nears its last note I raise my right hand and make the signal for the class to hold the last note. They do! I make the hand signal for the song to end, a sharp horizontal slice through the air with a pointed finger. The class follows my cue and ends the chorus exactly when my hand stops moving. Blown away, my heart is bursting with the wonder that is my life. I thank everyone and take the pictures.

Walking back to class, I realize I am creating my own reality. I am aware of living an awake dream. My Toltec teachers spoke of the ability to create your own reality — the internal intent reaching out to the external, initiating an event without knowing the outcome. Encountering this phenomenon, so intimately and perfectly, generates a moment I hope never to forget.

I go back to my writing class and pick up my things. I say goodbye to a few classmates I have been friendly with this past week. Most are going to lunch, but I know nothing can top what has just happened, and I decide it is time to leave Omega and walk to my car instead. I pull out of the campus on the same dirt road as Sister Alice with the week's adventures resonating inside me . . . all the way home.

Here
on the
paths to
everyday

I LOOK IN THE REFRIGERATOR BUT NOTHING APPEALS TO ME. I'VE BEEN UP FOR hours, meditating and writing with nothing but coffee, so now I'm famished. I decide to go to the bagel store. I don't even brush my teeth. If I'm going to have another cup of coffee with a warm bagel I don't want that minty, overly awake taste in my mouth. Just don't breathe on anybody, I tell myself as I hop into the minivan.

The line isn't too long, and I inhale the doughy bagel air. "I need a dozen," I tell the young man on the other side of the counter, "ten egg and two egg onion." A man next to me chuckles a little. "I know" I say, "that's the only kind the kids will eat." I look at the variety of bagels and silently shake my head. What a missed opportunity for the taste buds. But having bought various flavored bagels in the past, sesame, garlic, cinnamon raisin and black Russian, and watch them grow stale because they weren't the preferred egg bagel, I know to resist the urge for variety today.

The full bag of bagels smells like fresh bread with a bite of onion. The bag is warm, soft enough to give in a little when I hug it to my chest while struggling to open the van door with full hands. The only thing better than a fresh bagel is a fresh bagel with hazelnut coffee. I put the bag in the van and close the door. A Dunkin Donuts is about fifty feet away.

"Hallelujah!" I cry as I make my way to fresh brewed coffee.

The scent of hazelnut coffee mingles with the fresh bagel smell in the van on the way home. It is a short drive, which is good thing;

because the aroma is creating such a rumbling in my tummy that I would have reached in the bag and started eating if the ride was any longer.

I slice open two bagels and prepare one with cream cheese for Andrew and one with butter for Joe. The young man threw in a garlic bagel; the extra one that comes with a dozen.

The garlic bagel is softer than the egg onion I usually eat. I smell the cream cheese longingly but know not to put it on my bagel. Eleven years ago I developed an intolerance for dairy products. My bagel and cream cheese days are over. Butter is a weak substitute, and I suffer the loss of creamy, salty cheese every time I spread it on my son's bagel. Today is no different; I momentarily mourn the loss of the sensation of a warm, fragrant, chewy bagel wrapped around fluffy, creamy, white tart cream cheese going into my mouth; of biting down while the cream cheese oozes out to the corners of the slightly squeezed bagel, squeezed just enough to fit inside my mouth. I have to squeeze these bagels because they are big and yeasty, the bread is shot full of air; they give the appearance of lightness, though they can sit in my stomach like a brick if I eat too many, too often.

I spread the butter and try to be grateful for the fresh garlic bagel and not pine over lost cream cheese. I ask Joe and Andrew to eat with me on the upper deck that overlooks the backyard. Hazelnut coffee and bagel in hand, I climb up the back steps to the deck. I like sitting up here, especially now that I have the new bar set. The seats are higher, and I can see over the top railing. The old patio table and chairs were too low; every time I sat down the five-inch wide top deck rail blocked my view. As stupid as it sounds, the thousand dollars for the new set is worth the unobstructed view.

Looking out over the backyard, a familiar sense of satisfaction comes over me. I created that. I take in the light blue water of the oval shaped pool, surrounded by brown wood decking and six-foot high sea grass. The weeping pine tree with its serpentine shape, every year reaching farther down the landscaped bed surrounding the deck. The crape myrtle bush with its shiny green leaves and lilac like blooms at the far end of the rounded corner of the pool. The hostas on the other side with their long elegant flower stems slightly leaning over the side of the pool that gives the water a natural tropical illusion; the dense foliage of the pear trees behind the hostas that provide privacy from the houses to the east and north of us.

All of it and more I had designed and planted. There had been nothing there when we moved in; only one big empty grass lot for the previous owners' dogs to poop in. The previous owners were boat people and spent summers on the water. They didn't care about the backyard. But I did. I wanted a place to relax that was tranquil and reflected my taste. I wanted a place to sip an iced tea or glass of wine while I read a book. I created my own little oasis. But like most working moms, I don't visit too often. That's why I like the upper deck; I can gaze out and enjoy, even if it is only for a few minutes. I can look out and take in all that the view represents: creativity, tenacity, vision and luxury.

August 2002

A week after my writing workshop, I'm back at Omega with Joe. We liked Gurmukh's Kundalini Yoga sampler so much last year, we signed up for a whole weekend with her this summer. Never mind that Joe hasn't done yoga since that night one year ago; he is so enchanted with Gurmukh he wants to come back. I at least have been going to yoga about once a week at Grace's studio. But Grace's yoga is nothing like Kundalini yoga.

Kundalini yoga is an exercise in endurance. The postures and breathing and body motions seem to go on forever. The payoff is in stopping. Whoosh, the energy keeps moving, though my body is at rest. Finally, not moving, the body absorbs and then lets go the pulsating waves of energy that start within and radiate out beyond the skin. We wake up to chant at four-thirty in the morning. We sweat, meditate and listen to Gurmukh tell us that the opposite of love is not hate. It is fear.

She speaks of the agreements we keep with ourselves. She speaks of Martin Luther King Jr. and Mahatma Gandhi and all the people who gave their life for their truth. Her words reflect the message I received at Montsegur only two months ago.

I get up enough nerve to sit with Gurmukh and her husband at lunch and tell her how much her pre-yoga talks remind me of Don Miguel and the other teachers I have been working with.

"All spiritual paths lead to the same place," she explains. She is not pushing any particular path, only sharing the one she knows best. After a particularly grueling set of Kundalini exercises she asks the class to share what we are grateful for. I tell her that I feel grateful to feel gratitude, because when I feel grateful, I feel God.

Leaving the nirvana bubble of Omega behind, I jump back into the corporate tax season. It has been a long day at work in Manhattan, but I'm not as tired as I sometimes can be after a ten-hour day. I'm looking forward to meditating tonight. Everyone who is part of the on-line meditation group is supposed to meditate at the same time — nine at night. I have only sat once since the group was formed. I have been taking Adult Ed classes in Web design at night so I haven't been able to participate much since the group got started. Tonight will be tough, though; I won't be home until eight forty-five.

I kiss everyone hello and change into more comfortable clothes. I light some candles and make sure the door to the downstairs, where Joe and the boys are watching TV, is closed. I sit on a pillow on the floor with my legs crossed, my hands resting on my knees. I close my eyes and immediately feel breezes of energy blowing past me.

The energy feels like teeny-tiny particles vibrating at the same frequency. The cloud of vibration passes close by, and then another cloud vibrating at a different frequency swirls near me from the opposite direction. Within a few moments of sitting down a sea of energy winds surrounds me.

Pulled forward, the energies invite me to join in their dance. My breathing changes of its own accord, unfamiliarly inhaling and exhaling in a deep and pronounced way. Scared, excited and overwhelmed, I feel my heartbeat pop irregularly a few times. I pull myself back mentally and straighten my spine upward. I begin to scan the area for energy, focusing on what is happening outside my body. My head slowly moves from left to right, my concentration like the beam of light coming out of a lighthouse over a dark sea. Then I realize my head is not physically moving, that there is only a sensation of movement as I focus on the vibrations while in this hyper-sensitive state.

I do not think about doing any of this; I scan, as if this is the most natural thing to do while being swept away by alien energy clouds. Thankfully, the scanning activity calms me, and my heartbeat returns to normal. My breathing continues to be steady, deep, and not my own. The energy swirling around me floats and hovers near. I become aware of the pillow beneath my butt, my crossed legs with ankles resting on calves. From the waist down I feel solid and stable. From the waist up, however, there is a trend of lightness. The bottom half of my body is keeping my upper half from floating upward and outward. I can't help but be transfixed by the sensation of lightness, while at the same time being fascinated by the distinctly different sensation in another part of my body. Waist down is heavy, familiar, warm and fleshy. My abdomen and chest are light, expansive as if filled with helium. My arms bear little or no weight on my shoulders or knees. My hands, if not attached, would float up and hit the ceiling. My neck and head have almost dissolved. I cannot perceive a distinct boundary between my head and the energy surrounding me. Focusing on my physical body I feel myself become transparent from the waist up. I am no longer upset or overwhelmed. I experience the phenomenon of merging with whatever is out there and wait to see what will happen next.

After sitting immersed in my own transparency, I become aware of my surroundings again — the living room, the candlelight, the sound of the TV downstairs. My thoughts come slowly back to the familiar territory of wondering what I should eat this late at night? What do the boys need to do before I put them to bed? I open my eyes and wait for my body to respond to my directions to get up. Still feeling disconnected to the familiar room I see with my eyes, it takes a few more minutes to move. I get up and look at the clock. Thirty minutes have passed.

I know this sitting is different from all the rest. I didn't *do* anything. I didn't ask any questions; I didn't visualize any images to get me started. I wasn't looking for any answers. All I did was sit down and perceive. Something. Something not generated by me. Of that I am certain. I want to believe I have been invited by the energy beings to participate in a grand adventure. I realize there is a whole universe right here that I have not been tuned into — until tonight.

Almost a week later I am able to join the on-line meditation group again. At first I am preoccupied with maintaining good balance in my meditation posture. From the waist up I tend to drift forward and then tilt my head back. My thoughts circle around how I'm not sitting right. Then I shift my position and refocus, but eventually I drift forward again.

After fifteen minutes of drifting and straightening, I have the sensation of a pole going through the top of my head to the base of my spine. I align my back with this virtual support and am grounded and centered.

I wonder when I am done meditating alone in my living room, if the energy of the group is helping me out or the thought of being with others is helping. Or is something else out there wanting to help? Either way, my meditation posture is not an issue anymore.

Being part of a virtual group doesn't reach the intimacy of the companionship I felt with the women on our France adventure, so I convince Joe that we should go to Don Miguel's Circle of Fire weekend when I find out some of them will be there. Now, at the end of the summer, I find myself sitting with forty people in a large conference room on Asilomar Conference Grounds in California.

Faith is the subject, faith healing in particular. I'm not comfortable with the drift of the workshop, but once a workshop begins I almost never leave. This is out of fear of offending the workshop leader. I hope I can listen and not have to actually do anything. I originally signed up for the workshop because Mother Sarita, Don Miguel's mother, was supposed to be here.

Mother Sarita is a ninety-two year-old mother of thirteen and has been a bonafide faith healer for almost forty years. But I am not surprised when they announced Mother Sarita is not here. They did advertise 'health permitting' and ninety-two is a precarious age to be flying around the country. What is astonishing is that Don Miguel is here. He was in a coma after his third heart attack only a few months ago. During the opening ceremony he told everyone that it was his mother that kept him here. Her will alone brought him back from death. He was ready for the next step, the next journey, but Mom called him back.

Yeah, it would have been nice to meet Mother Sarita because I am familiar with a healer's power. I was lucky enough to experience firsthand the light but profound touch of Rita's hand. It has been nine months since Rita's hand touched my temple. I settle in and listen, even if I don't know what the hell I'm doing in a faith healing workshop on a Saturday afternoon in Monterey, California.

The workshop leader says she isn't fancy in her faith healing; she only knows one way to do it and that is with love. She says it is an act of faith that she is even standing before us now. Her path has led her here. That when we are invited to participate in life by others, more enlightened, spiritually experienced people, we should respond with our bigger self, not our little self. That is, respond with the larger view you have about yourself but don't admit to. Don't let that little version of yourself that you live with most of the time make you miss life's opportunities and invitations. That is faith: faith in life and faith in yourself.

The healer then asks everyone to close their eyes. She leads the group in a meditation to draw power from the earth. She tells us to call our own name within our mind. Karyn, Karyn, I call. I feel off balance for a moment as my name echoes internally in my expanded state of mind. A peculiar exercise, calling my own name and waiting for a response . . . I get one.

Now we are asked to put our called selves aside. To do faith healing, the healer explains, you must be a pure channel, let yourself move out of the way, so that healing energy can move through you. This is extremely difficult to do, but I give it a try, not really sure if I am successful or not. Next she has us imagine that we are growing roots down into the center of the earth and drawing on Mother Earth's strength and love. She tells us to fill ourselves with the energy of the mother.

I hear some moaning, and the temperature in the room goes up a few degrees. I definitely feel warmer and can at least imagine the power of the earth coming up my legs and into the rest of my body. The healer asks if people are ready to release this energy, and many people respond with a resounding yes. I am not one of them. I don't even know if I have energy to release or if I am merely going along with the show.

A man and a woman that need healing are brought to the front of the room. The woman is helped onto a table. Volunteers are asked to surround the table with the other faith healer whose name I have already forgotten. The gentleman is laid out on the floor with more volunteers placed around him.

Oh, good, I conclude. I can sit back and watch. But before I see any action, the rest of us are told to pair up and face each other.

An older woman on my right looks at me and nods her head, and we turn our chairs towards each other.

Oh, shit, I say to myself, now what!

The healer instructs one person to go first and give a healing touch to the other. Release the energy that has been drawn up from the earth and use it to heal and comfort the one in front of you.

Now I'm in trouble. Drawing energy from the earth had been a tepid affair, and I am certainly not bursting with unrealized energy ready to shoot from my fingertips. Damn, I hope this lady wants to go first; I have no idea what I am supposed to do.

She motions she will start and places one leg on either side of my closed legs.

I close my eyes and try to relax.

The woman touches me lightly on the arms, shoulders and head.

Her touch is comforting and pleasantly well intended. I can do this, I tell myself and calm down somewhat before we exchange roles.

When the group is told to switch, I open my thighs to surround the woman's legs with my own. As I open my legs, they had been pressed together tightly to allow the other woman's legs to reach around me, I immediately become aware of a sensation in my womb. The sensation continues and grounds itself to encompass my whole base. I feel a deep subtle vibration in the space below my belly button and above my butt.

I look over at the woman and place my hands on her thighs that are directly in front of my womb and between my spread legs. I start to cry with the unexpected tenderness I feel for this woman, this stranger. I am so startled by my own emotions that I can't do anything but stay in that position for a few moments. I mentally project my message of love and tenderness towards the woman while placing my hands on her shoulders and arms. After a minute I decide to send a message with the love, a message that the woman is Divine, as we all are Divine. I tell her with my silent intent that she is okay and is capable of being a Divine creature.

I notice that she has her palms placed down on top of her knees. I get a distinct notion that I should turn her palms upward. I reach for the woman's hands and turn them over. As I do this I receive an image of Christ's hands after the crucifixion. The image doesn't startle me as much as puzzle me. I don't think about Jesus too often, and the crucifixion is not my favorite part of Christianity. To be honest, I'm not sure I believe it. But at this point I am following instinct and decide not to question the image, but go with the odd feeling/instructions/impressions that are evolving during this unexpected turn of events.

I hold the image of Christ's hands in my mind, and I know I should touch the woman's palms in the spot where the nails would have been if they were Jesus' hands. This is unnerving; I know exactly where to touch her, not like in the beginning of the session when I had no idea of where to start or what to do.

I cup my hands on the outside of the woman's hands and press either thumb at the same time into the soft center of each palm. As the woman's flesh gives in slightly to the pressure of my thumbs, I hear the message that the woman doesn't need to suffer anymore. That she is loved and everything will be okay. Why I thought this woman might be suffering I'm not sure, but, again, I send a message that seems instinctual, a thought that exists in the moment, but not formulated prior to the second it comes into my awareness. At that moment the woman gasps and begins to cry. Her whole body relaxes as the tears roll down her face. After a few moments when I feel more like myself I stand up and lean over my partner and kiss her on both cheeks and say, "I love you."

She gazes up at me and, with watery eyes, replies, "I know."

After a moment or two I begin to feel as I did at the start of the session; what do I do now? I am done. I look around the room and notice that the person on the table is a different woman, someone I know. I want to go up to the table and join some of the other people who are healing her. I look over at my partner and see her leaning back, eyes slightly closed with a contented smile on her face. She has placed each hand on top of my knees; I cannot easily extract myself without disturbing her. Oh, well, I guess she isn't ready to give up a good thing. I resolve to stay seated as long as my partner wants to remain in that space. I look over at the table again and can't help wondering what would happen if I tried laying my hands again. Would I channel the same energy I just experienced? Would incredible love pour out of me again? I won't find out today; the workshop is ending and suddenly I am extremely hungry.

Enter, rejoice and come in

I DECIDE TO TALK ABOUT MY ANGEL IN MY SECOND SUMMER SERVICE. WHEN WE moved into our second house I was lucky enough to have the time and money to decorate. With our first house, childproofing was the main goal. The boys were both in elementary school when we moved into our second house. I was working full time, not out of choice, but nevertheless, the extra hours of work brought in extra money. My spending on the new house purposefully offset my unhappiness at being forced back into a full time position by my boss. I didn't have any formal training in decorating. I had never been all that interested. But now with a blank canvas, so to speak, I was ready to bring forth my vision of a home.

Because I worked during the day and didn't have much time to go shopping, I flipped through catalogs at night. I gazed at pictures of bronze sconces, imagining the soft candlelight against my recently painted cappuccino hued dining room walls. Multi-textured pillows of deep maroon with contrasting teal tassels danced before my eyes nightly as I pictured how it would all come together. Boxes would arrive by UPS while I was at work, and I'd come home to a mini Christmas at least once a week. I joked with my friends that I was spending my way out of a depression brought on by working a full-time job I did not want.

One night, flipping through a Spiegel catalog, I came upon a picture of an angel in a white Grecian tunic. She has two huge wings framing her arms, shoulders, head and back. Her arms are held out slightly from her body giving a subtle impression of acceptance. Even though her hands are not shown, the position of her arms lets me know that her palms are facing open and outward in a quiet, beseeching manner. I'm drawn to the inward focus of her steady gaze.

The angel had caught my eye, but I immediately dismissed the painting as anything that would compliment our new home. I flipped through the rest of the catalog and put it aside. But the image of the angel would not leave me. I found myself going back to that catalog again and again to look at the angel, only to dismiss the idea of hanging her on my wall each time I gave in to the urge to look at her. She had a look of innocence that intrigued me, but the whole idea of an angel seemed too Catholic. Angels, crosses, statues of saints were all conspicuously absent in my parents and grandparents homes. Brought up as a Protestant, any fondness for a religious relic was akin to idolatry. But the past didn't matter, the angel called to me night after night.

Finally I decided to buy her in order to end the indecision and the tugging at my heart. I rationalized that if the picture looked tacky, I could always hang it in the bathroom. Nobody in the family could object to an angel in the washroom. I knew I couldn't *not* buy the angel; I was too disconcerted every time I tried to dismiss the picture and move on with my decorating.

When the painting arrived and I unwrapped her, I felt as if I had found a long lost friend. She was immediately familiar, and now she graces the wall that joins my dining and living room. Her presence is comforting and inspiring, especially when I become aggravated at the multitude of everyday modern annoyances. There is something more about her — a quality hard to explain in words. She speaks directly to my heart. She has an ability to evoke feelings of devotion and tenderness, vague unclassifiable feelings of yearning and wonderment. It wasn't until my experience on the Long Island Rail Road that I realized that God was reaching out to me through the angel.

I found my angel in Omega's bookstore a few years later when Joe and I attended Don Miguel's workshop the summer of 2001. She was exactly the same but in another form. She graced the cover of a journal. I bought her again, and I've filled her pages with my adventures, lessons and yearnings. My angel is famous. When I opened the journal and read the cover title I found out the original painting hangs in the

Smithsonian Institution and was painted by Abbott Handerson Thayer. The painting is simply titled *Angel*.

September 2002

I meditate at night four or five days out of the week, able to sit for longer periods with greater ease. The major obstacle is settling down in the house and not rushing because of the household chores waiting to be done. Most nights have been peaceful. Tonight I feel and then see a presence in my living room while meditating.

Well, who is this? I ask myself, as I watch a youngish bearded man sit down on the floor across from me.

The candles I had lit earlier on the coffee table illuminate his face and hair. At first he acts as though he is going to join me in meditation. But soon after I become sensitive to his presence, I find myself wondering about the significance of his visit. His corporal presence dissipates as my curiosity increases, and eventually he fades into the candlelight.

The initial realization of another presence and the vision of the young man remain with me for the rest of the evening. The meeting is distinct and not like anything else I have experienced while meditating. I hope he comes back. He was only with me for a moment or two.

Walking down the Avenue of the Americas on my way home early in September, I let my head empty of the day's accomplishments and notice the people on the bustling city sidewalk. As I weave in and out of the pedestrian traffic I appreciate the unique bubble of reality every person inhabits. So many souls, each one locked up and isolated within a body. Each individual seems utterly impervious to the person next to them, yet somehow we all are connected. Connected by our common perception of this place and this moment.

Sometimes a connection is made. Usually people who are passing each other on a New York City street will not look each other in the eye. When I do make eye contact I notice one of two possibilities. Often one of us will look away quickly, as if we have been caught doing something we shouldn't. Or, more rarely, the person whose eye I have caught will recognize that a connection has been made, and we will acknowledge each other. The acknowledgement of a connection opens a brief dialogue between us. This is the purest type of communication, no words or desire for anything else is present — just a simple recognition of each other's being.

Now I feel a link, whether the other person acknowledges the connection or not. I feel a bond to them regardless. Not only that, an aching compassion for strangers will wash over me at the most inopportune times. It happens today as I descend the steps at the Seventh Avenue entrance to Penn Station. I move among hundreds of people and tears fill my eyes as I melt into a sea of souls. Lightheaded, my body turns rubbery from the tender vulnerability I experience being part of the immense wake of human animation.

What a fool — here am I, teary eyed and mushy in the middle of rush hour in one of the busiest train stations on the planet. What in the world is wrong with me? I wonder, zigzaging my blurry self to the train platform. What a noodle head, I sniff, embarrassed at the thought of anyone noticing my weakened state. What kind of New Yorker am I? I chastise myself. I board the train, and the wave of exposed passion subsides when I settle into the hard vinyl seat. I don't act like this most days. I'm sure something is triggering the emotional submersion, something subtle, but I haven't figured out what. Yet. As embarrassed as I am, I cherish the experience. I love loving these strangers. It feels good. It feels right.

I receive electronic chain mail quite often these days, especially from my sister Lynn. She lives in Connecticut with her mother, my father's second wife, and her grandmother. My father died when she was a baby, but we stay in touch, mostly by e-mail. Most of what she and others send is deleted. Threats of bad luck are dismissed with a keystroke. Chain e-mail is more dreadful than the junk I used to get as a kid. The ease with which we can annoy each other electronically is disturbing. Today I keep what she sends; then forward the anonymous prayer on.

> I asked God to take away my habit.
> God said, No.
> It is not for me to take away,
> But for you to give up.

I asked God to make my handicapped child whole.
God said, No.
His spirit is whole, his body is only temporary

I asked God to grant me patience
God said, No.
Patience is a byproduct of tribulations;
It isn't granted, it is learned.

I asked God to give me happiness.
God said, No.
I give you blessings; Happiness is up to you.

I asked God to spare me pain.
God said, No.
Suffering draws you apart from worldly cares,
And brings you closer to me.

I asked God to make my spirit grow.
God said, No.
You must grow on your own!
But I will prune you to make you fruitful.

I asked God for all things that I might enjoy life.
God said, No.
I will give you life, so that you may enjoy all things.

I ask God to help me Love others,
As much as God loves me.

God said . . . Ahhhh, finally you have the idea.

Working more hours in the city, I struggle again to maintain a regular meditation practice. On the nights I work — I feel guilty taking more time away from my family. On the nights I don't work outside my home — I enjoy being part of our homey fabric and resist pulling myself away from my cozy cocoon to explore what may turn out to be nothing.

Tonight I take the time to light a candle and sit cross-legged on my pillows in my living room. Tonight my mind floats easily into the soup. My thoughts are airy and easy to dismiss, once I recognize that I am preoccupied with them. I stay aware for any subtle shifts of energy or presences or unusual body sensations. I sit for fifteen minutes or so and figure no fireworks tonight; time for tea and bed.

As I consider ending my sitting, heaviness descends in the area between my eyebrows. I see quite distinctly stone pillars with Egyptian hieroglyphics. But the image isn't the only thing that captures my attention; it is the sensation of the pillars between my eyebrows. I view the columns through binoculars turned the wrong way, so I am looking inward and see primeval stone pillars. I feel them, heavy, coldly dense and ancient. I assume there is a message here, but since I don't read hieroglyphics, I am literally left in the dark.

I can't help but think something projected the columns onto my mind. The pillars were there from no where. No thought of mine preceded it. The sensation is so distinct and new, I can't believe I produced it myself. But I can't believe the occurrence was from outside of me, either. Such is the spiritual path, almost as bad as my therapist saying, "And what do you think?" I want answers; I already have plenty of questions, thank you. Well, at least now I know why they call the area between the eyebrows the third eye. Tonight it certainly was just that.

Commuting from the city means giving up group meditation most weekdays. So when I finally find the time to go I'm disappointed when the Buddhist meditation teacher, who comes every other week to my fellowship, couldn't make it herself. Instead our pastor leads the first silent meditation, and I volunteer to lead the walking meditation. I have been taught that having no expectations during meditation is important, and I certainly didn't have any with the Pastor leading the meditation in our meeting room with a creaking ceiling fan overhead.

The last sitting of the night, as soon as the meditation bowl is tapped, I'm 'off'. Normal thoughts are not possible — I am flying like an eagle over a forest. I don't flap my arms like wings; instead I soar, caught in a linear vortex of energy. The flight is so THERE and vivid; even a 3-D IMAX movie cannot compare.

When the meditation ends I speculate that I have tapped into the energy brought by an Inter-Faith Alliance visitor, a man studying to be a Rabbi. The gentleman has a clear presence that I have not noticed in other sittings with this group. I have never seen him at meditation before but have participated in one of his workshops. I don't know. All I know is what I experienced. And I wish it would happen more often.

Do not be conformed to this world

THE IDEA OF ACCEPTING *WHAT IS* BOTHERS ME. I MEDITATE ON THE BUDDHIST principle of acceptance and eventually come to see the wisdom of doing what I can to change what I find objectionable, while accepting *what is* now. I'm able to discern that accepting does not mean doing nothing. Rather, acceptance means after I take action, whether this is extending compassionate energy for others, participating in social justice projects or becoming involved politically — I accept *what is* now. I do not spend more energy resisting what is. I respect the existence of all creation. I have come to appreciate that acceptance does not mean I can't change anything. But I must accept what is, to have peace within myself.

November 2002

Ask yourselves the question: Why am I here? Then look for the answer in a dream and set the intent to remember the dream.

That is the assignment we are given tonight.

I wake up every hour without a single recollection of a dream. Each time, before I fall back to sleep, I reset my intent to find out why I am here.

As if seen through the lens of a video camera, I find myself walking down a marina dock to the end of the pier. A rowboat is tied to the end of the dock, and I walk close enough to see two dead bodies inside the open bow. Bloody and mutilated, they obviously have been murdered.

The next sequence in my viewfinder is inside the cabin of a luxury yacht. The bedroom cabin is decorated with opulent red and gold fabrics. There are two dead bodies on the floor; one is decapitated. The body with a head comes back to life and attempts to reattach the decapitated body's head so it can be reanimated also. As I watch the gruesome scene, I understand clearly that I was the perpetrator of the first murder as well as the person murdered. Somehow I remained conscious enough to come back in the dead body in the luxury boat.

I resurrected myself!

The gruesome but fascinating movie fades to black as I wake up next to Joe. "It's eight fifteen. We overslept!" I say urgently. "We never sleep this late!" We jump into some clothes so we can eat breakfast before they put the food away. My intent was so well set that both of us slept until the answer, in a dream, appeared.

I am here this weekend to find out how to bridge this life to the next. Maybe not only bridge this life to the next but be conscious enough to pick an environment of my own choosing. A sitcom theme song fills my mind. *Moving on Up* takes on a whole new meaning. After breakfast I am compelled to share my dream when the teacher tells the oldest member of the group that her purpose as a teacher is to prepare us for the end of this life. Prepare us, so that we are not afraid of the transition death represents.

We explore the relationship between trust and control on the Saturday afternoon following my dream during our Wisdom Group weekend. As a child and a teenager, I often confused my sympathy for family members with a lack of personal boundaries. I learned not to trust my feelings because most of the adults in my life told me that everything is okay. Obviously everything was not okay, but as a young dependent child, I believed the adults and disavowed my feelings. During our second sitting, I come to realize that I believed that I could not trust others because of my past inability as a child to keep healthy boundaries. I held the belief that I could not trust myself, either; that's how I learned to control the situation at hand in order to feel safe. I saw my habit of setting up whatever I would be doing next, so that I would know how to respond ahead of time. Doing this, I didn't have to trust the people I was with or my feelings.

I realize while sitting that my beliefs no longer serve me. I am older and wiser, and I don't have to get into any compromising situations as long as I stay aware of what and why I am doing something. I can trust myself to have compassion for others and maintain healthy boundaries at the same time. My desire is to be aware in every moment and to have the ability to choose in that moment what I want to do, based on my feelings and my integrity. I do not want to set up my life and miss the authenticity of living every new moment. I want to be present, aware and choosing in every minute of my life.

December 2002

The on-line meditation group is now known as Mystica. I take a few minutes off from work to write about death and identity in response to an e-mail. I suspect that what I do now creates my future, and as I become more conscious, what I do in the future leaves markers for me to follow in the present, which is my future's past. In essence, I am guiding myself with my future self. We all do this but are at different levels of consciousness; either we pick up on the clues we leave for ourselves, or we stumble around in the dark until we encounter someone who can shed some light. In the end, we are really all one consciousness splintered into separate illusions of past, present and future.

I illustrate my feelings in the e-mail by explaining how I see my children. I hardly ever refer to them as my sons in the biblical sense of 'flesh of my flesh'. Ever since they were infants I've felt as if they were unique beings in my care. Growing up, going to school and socialization seemed to make them less unique somehow. Not in actuality, but the process somehow cloaked their light of being.

Writing about Andrew and Garrett in my Mystica e-mail leads me further away from work and back to a time when none of these thoughts filled my head — a time when my life revolved around the two little boys that enchant me still. I can still remember pulling into the driveway and seeing Andrew filling up empty two-liter Coke bottles with the hose. He is so intent he doesn't even look up to see that I am home. I watch as he fills the bottle, picks it up, moves it over a few feet and then pours out the water onto the pavement. I wait until he is done to go over and give him a kiss. He grunts a deep little growl of recognition and goes back to his hose and bottles. The bottle he carries is as big as his chubby toddler arms. He will continue in this way for twenty minutes, completely absorbed in a task that has an importance only he is aware of. That is Andrew, my first child. Always Andrew, never Andy, actively intent, absorbed, curious and self possessed. I never felt that he came from Joe or me. He always seemed to be the essence of Andrew from the very beginning. He doesn't seem to belong to anyone but himself. He was never afraid to go to anybody, never shy or hiding behind my legs like some kids do. No, Andrew met the world head on from the time he could crawl. It seemed his confidence in being alive made me an extraordinarily confident mother. I never doubted my abilities as a mother once. I almost never called the pediatrician, my mother or other older, more experienced, moms. I knew I would do the right thing for Andrew, and he thrived.

Andrew loved having a baby brother. He couldn't say baby so he called Garrett Boo-Boo when Garrett came home from the hospital. The most enjoyable phrase Andrew came up with was during Garrett's feedings. Andrew would point to the bottle and say, "Boo-Boo's baba." That was a keeper phrase. He loves having a brother, but Andrew learned early on to share his mother. He was only fifteen months old when Garrett was born. I can see Andrew squatting down in front of the TV watching Muppet Babies and then looking up at me on the couch feeding Boo-Boo. His eyes say, "That used to be me up there in your arms." He would look at me for a moment with longing, but being Andrew, he turns back to the TV, not complaining or demanding, only acceptance of his change in status.

I remember looking down at Garrett while nursing and being drawn to the deepest, grayest eyes I have ever seen on an infant. Garrett's eyes tell a tale of antiquity. Looking into his eyes I know what people mean by an old soul. Garrett has been around; those eyes knew. I am convinced Garrett's soul had been there and done that.

Years later when Garrett is six, he tells me that he knows things. "What things?" I ask.

"Just stuff, I know them," he says. "How do I know?" he asks me.

I'm at a loss to explain. Instead I tell him everybody's brain works differently. I believe he has memories of times past but doesn't know where or how they belong. By the time he is ten he doesn't even remember asking me that question or telling me that he knows things.

I guess we are not supposed to remember. Too bad. I would love to know what he thought he knew.

The next day's Mystica e-mails reveal our dismay with the state of the world. A woman's lament about the Bush missile fiasco and her corresponding sadness concerning the current political situation reminds me that maybe I should be doing something. I agree with her that the U.S. foreign policy is taking the country in the wrong direction. I disagree with the current administration on almost every issue. I've marched in Washington three times in the past, and I've run for office, but since turning inward and forty, I don't have the desire to turn my anger into protest. When I berate myself for doing nothing to stop the madness, I remind myself to do what I can, but accept *what is.*

Listening to *The Way of the Peaceful Warrior* by Dan Millman on tape on my way to work the next morning, I follow his theme that there is only now. I do not wish to spend time thinking about what I think I should do about world affairs. I want to do what I can in the moment. At this moment, while the U.S. drops bombs, I understand I cannot stop it. I do hope that I have the strength in the moment, when that time comes, to get on a bus, to march, or to write a letter or take whatever right action presents itself. But until that moment is now, I do not want to create negative emotion or energy judging past and possible future events.

I remember when I used to get more worked up about political events. Sometimes there was positive energy, like the time I had to give my first political speech. I believed everything I said and campaigned on. Still do. If I run again, I want to be out there for the right reasons, and I can't do that until I understand my motivations and myself more clearly. But I will always remember that first speech. I can see myself with Joe at the Suffolk County nominating convention in 1996.

I am waiting to speak in front of hundreds of committee people, scores of politicians, and the press. I have never given a political speech in my life, yet I am ready — eager, in fact. I have practiced this speech twenty or thirty times in front of the mirror. The speech is short, heartfelt and damn good. The speech is good, because I believe every word. It's good for me, and I hope it is good for them. Not that it matters; my outrage has to come out. I need to hear myself speak aloud the words that lead me to run for office when I have no idea what to do or how to do it. Yet. I need to speak; to convey my message to these people I don't know but will need in the weeks to come.

My mouth is dry. I force myself to salivate. I don't want to choke on my own words. I try to listen to the other nominated candidates, but it's useless. All I can do is hold my self together. All my cells are buzzing; they feel like they will fly off in every direction, leaving me disintegrated. The only thing holding me together is my will. My will is barely reining in the buzzing, vibrating pieces of matter that is me.

"Disintegrate later," I say to myself, "your three minutes of fame is coming up." I listen and realize I am going to be next. The chairman of the Democratic Party in Suffolk County is introducing me. I rise to take my place at the podium. Unbelievably my legs move forward and don't collapse underneath me. The view from the podium brings a new perspective. I grip the podium sides and take a moment and look out over the crowd. A heady feeling settles over me as I realize I could get used to this. I begin with, "Hello," and as I pause the crowd answers back "Hello!" I'm won over and smile.

I deliver my speech as memorized. It is short, heartfelt and damn good. I go unconvinced that it could be different. The crowd applauds loudly, and I can see the surprise in their faces. I am not what they expected. I'm not what I expected. I am smiling, ecstatically and emphatically, buzzing as I cross the stage to take my seat.

The chairman rises to shake my hand, clearly pleased to be seen with me on stage.

Yes, a new perspective. I could get used to this.

I am being driven into an unknown land

THE FLIGHT TO MEXICO CITY IS UNEVENTFUL, AND JOE AND I GET THROUGH customs without a hitch. The meeting place, Freedom Cantina, is on our right. Walking closer, I notice a woman squatting amongst a pile of luggage outside the entrance of the restaurant. Her tight curly hair encircles a clear, pale, enchanting face. She looks like a modern day angel with her translucent face and blue jeans. I can't place where I have seen her before but am almost certain we have met. I can't stop looking at her as we approach. Everything else in the airport recedes from my attention as I am drawn closer and detect the look of wanting to belong on her face. Her eyes are pleading for someone to notice her pain. I fall in love as I drink in all of her — her face, her eyes, her tender yearning for connection.

Airport activity becomes less muted as I become more conscious of my surroundings. I realize she must be part of our group and introduce myself. I ask her if we have met before. She tells us her name and, "Yes, we met in November in New Jersey at the last Wisdom Group." I am drawn to her, but after a few minutes of conversation other members of the group arrive, and I get caught up in the excitement of a new adventure with new people. I ecstatically greet Gloria and Susan, fellow seekers from our France journey, and the three of us head out to find the restroom. I stroll down the airport concourse with an arm around each woman's waist and can't remember being this happy in a long time.

Coming back from the restroom we walk separately; the concourse has become crowded with travelers. I look at the people as they pass by or as I pass them while they stand waiting to board their planes. As I gaze into their faces, I acknowledge a supple, warm attachment to each one, as if I somehow know them from before. Their faces are familiar in a non-specific way. I fall in love with each and every face my eyes see. A buoyancy of light filled emotion fluffs and sustains me. Trance like, floating along a not quite real open hallway, I am only slightly aware of the multitude of colors, noises and movements surrounding me. My attention is filled with the delicious feeling of compassion I have for everyone as I make my way through the busy thoroughfare.

I must have looked dazed. Gloria reaches out and touches my arm and warns me to watch out. There is a baggage tram right behind me, and I move out of the way. The airport is an airport again as I come down to earth on my way back to the restaurant to join the others for a snack before boarding the bus to Teotihuacan.

The group gathers every night to share, meditate and receive a lesson. The only time I question whether my journey is spiritual is when a few people share their experience of visions, emotional meltdowns and weightlessness. Not me, though. Most of the trip is calm, deep and relatively uneventful as far as mysticism is concerned. I exist on a different emotional plane than I do at home, and the ease of being with everyone is a complete joy. While I don't have any visions or ride waves of energy, I do experience a distinct clarity in the messages I receive at the different sites we visit during the day. There are no voices to hear, but the message makes itself known through words. The quality of my awareness when the message enters my mind is unmistakable although indescribable. The message is not thought — it is made known. The messages are complete, clear and distinct from all other thoughts. In writing class, Lynda Barry referred to the experience as the Unthought Known. A phrase she attributes to Christopher Bollas and his book *The Shadow of the Object: Psychoanalysis of the Unthought Known*. I don't need to read the book to know what he is talking about.

In the plateau of Earth, the metaphorical belly of the feathered serpent, I sit quietly on a rock. I decide to try my meditation technique and send a question out to the universe and let go. I worry that I should be doing more to help my part of the world become aware of the spiritual nature of life. I especially wonder if I am supposed to quit my secular job and take up more charitable endeavors. Part of me believes that I have leadership abilities. My experiences over the last eighteen months are pointing to an accelerated and clear path towards helping others or contributing in a leadership role. Another part of me thinks the idea is pure ego; that my need for recognition and my competitive tendencies are at the root of my aspirations.

I ask the Universe, "Am I a leader or meant to lead?"

BAM the answer comes back immediately. *"Just be of service, the rest will follow. It doesn't matter as long as your actions are done in service. You don't have to make a big decision. When in the moment, take actions of service."*

The message is as clear as getting directions in a car equipped with GPS. Take a right, go three blocks and make a left at Smith Street. Although I do not 'hear' a voice, the messenger leaves a feminine impression. Elated, I feel a weight being lifted from my shoulders. I can choose in the moment to be of service. No difficult decisions to make, no sacrificing a comfortable standard of living for sackcloth and ashes. Choose to be of service when the opportunity arises. I can do that.

The following day the teacher leads the group into the area known as the Home of the Masters. She stops at a small grotto covered with a protective grate of steel bars. The grotto's opening is at ground level so the people closest kneel on the floor while peering in. We are instructed to say a prayer or meditate, then move on, so that the people behind us can come closer and kneel after us.

As I kneel before the ancient stone grotto, I have a strong desire to bow my head. I bow my head and cup my hands on my knees. My hands are my begging bowl, and I beseech the masters to put into my bowl whatever they wish to give me. My neck turns rubbery as I bow my head lower. With each breath my head rests closer to my heart, and I surrender completely to the presence of Divine intelligence. After a few moments I rise and let others approach. We are guided to sit in silence in the courtyard, while everyone has a chance to visit and meditate in the sacred area of the Masters. The wall behind my back and the ground beneath my legs support my full body weight as I let all resistance go. I have never felt so peaceful in my life. I could stay here forever — at peace, resting and unquestioning.

Luckily we remain in the courtyard for some time. A heart surgeon is so overcome by what he has experienced that he is unable to get off the ground. He is on his back and seemingly unaware of his surroundings. After twenty minutes, several assistants get him on his feet. I don't know if the surrender and the peace are related, but I don't care. I marvel that I was physically able to relax my neck to the point where my head actually reached my heart. I have never achieved such elasticity in my neck before. My neck is the stiffest part of my body, and I regularly get adjusted at the chiropractor.

Our day is not over as we are led on a fifty minute silent walk to Tetitla. According to the Toltecs, Smokey Mirror was the founder of Toltec University in Teotihuacan, and Tetitla was his home. The first area we visit is an open courtyard with a stone stage. The wall at the back of the stage is an ancient mural protected by steel bars. We line up facing the stage, where we peer through the bars at the mural.

I examine the paintings, contemplating the story they represent. The drawings are a mix of Native South American art and Egyptian pictography. Nothing appears special about the ancient site to me, and I lay my head on my crossed arms resting on the stage. I lean my body against the cool stone, and a second later I receive a message. "*There needs to be a new mythology for a new era of light.*" I did not ask a question this time, but the message was as clear as the message I received the day before.

I move away from the stage and wait to be escorted to the room where everyone is now sitting. The teacher comes for me, and we enter a small area where half of the group is sitting on the floor facing one wall; the other half is facing the opposite wall. The backs of people facing opposite ways are leaning against each other for support. Placed up front next to the far wall, sitting sideways; I face the people sitting in the front row instead of the wall. Joe is closest to me and next to him is Gloria. There is a four inch raised partition running from the front wall to the back. I sit down on the ridge and open my legs wide for balance and support.

I let go thoughts questioning why we were placed in this particular configuration. I slip and stay in a light meditative state until I notice heavy breathing and gasping near me. I turn my head and look straight into two huge eyes. The eyes belong to the ancient bird painted on the front wall. I instantly recognize the bird that appeared to me when I journeyed with the Shaman at Omega this past summer. Painted centuries ago on a ruin wall in Teo is my sacred space protector, my hawk. Pleasantly surprised, I smile at the hawk with its wings spread wide and its huge, oversized eyes and wonder how on earth I didn't notice the painting when I first walked in and sat down next to it.

Joe does not want to wait for the last day to climb the Pyramid of the Sun. He persuades me to go with him alone after dinner — to climb the pyramid we have been looking at through the restaurant window every afternoon. When we get to the top of the Pyramid of the Sun we take a few minutes to meditate. Exhilarated by the view, my mind refuses to settle down. Attempts to focus are fruitless. Finally I ask what were the builders of this magnificent structure all about? For what purpose was the effort of building a perch so high above all else?

"FREEDOM!" is shouted back to me.

I become conscious with this word; the new mythology is freedom — to be free! Yes! Yes! Freedom! Give me freedom or give me death; my favorite American Revolutionary quote. My exhilaration quickly gives way to worry. Idealist movements always screw up, backfire, because somebody becomes a leader driven by ego and thousands follow — and the message is manipulated and distorted.

"Walk lightly, walk lightly upon this earth," the message from the Circle of Fire comes to me. How do I walk lightly? I ask, rather informally, more rumination than a real question.

"FREEDOM, PERSONAL FREEDOM," is shouted back at me. "FREEDOM FROM ALL TYRANNY." Whether the tyranny is personal demons, unconscious habit, cultural constraints, religious dogma or an oppressive government. Only when a person is truly free and aware are they able to choose in every moment. When that happens? There is no leader who can corrupt, no government that can harness multitudes to engage in warfare and oppression. No religion or culture can restrict an individual (who chooses in every moment with awareness) from creating the dream that is his or her life.

Still chilly on our last morning visiting the site, the group meditates at the hotel before we make our way to the pyramids. I close my eyes and listen to the teacher's voice as she uses the metaphor of a film projector and projection screen to describe our waking living dream that we call life. She tells us that we are the light that projects the film. The film is our beliefs, stories and emotions that make up our lives. We project onto the big white screen; the big white screen that represents the rest of the world. We are all projecting ourselves out to the blank canvas that is reality. We view the world through our projections.

I envision the picture painted for us. I see the light shining down from me, illuminating flickering images that fall onto a huge white screen. Suddenly, as the white projection screen fills my vision, a huge tear appears. I'm startled; nobody mentioned anything about ripping apart the screen or the world it represents. The vision is no longer of my own making. Fascinated, if there is no screen to project onto, what is there? No boundaries? No frame for existence? Compelling, scary questions. I try to look through the tear to see what is beyond the screen, but I cannot hold onto the vision, and the scene fades to black by the time the meditation is over.

When sharing our impressions of Teo before we re-enter the world we temporarily left behind, I tell my companions that we project onto the screen now, but in the future we won't need to. That somehow this is tied to the awareness of our own Divinity. The prospect of creating a collective reality differently is exciting to me. I want to explore how. I want to know what replaces our current frame of reference. I want to know what is going to rock our world.

Every
morning
the world
is created

S̲ITTING AT HOME IN MY LIVING ROOM WITH J̲OE, I̲ BEGIN BY VISUALIZING OUR upcoming trip to California for the Easter Celebration with Don Miguel and Mother Sarita. We will be visiting Rita and Gloria too, but I am planning the trip so the boys can meet Don Miguel. Due to his last heart attack nobody knows how long he will be with us, and I want the boys to meet the man who changed our lives and whose picture sits on our coffee table at home.

An expanded state of mind comes easily this morning. My body begins to buzz soon after, and the next thing I know I am a point of light in space with other points of light talking with a teacher. Apparently I have dropped into the middle of a teaching session. The teacher projects the idea that everything is perception and creation. What prevents us from feeling joy and creating only beauty and being in love is that we keep getting sucked into our little selves, and the world perceived is at that constricted level.

"What is that world?" I ask. "Is it physical, mental images or what?"

I want to understand the relationship between being a point of light and the world I experience through my senses. I receive the answer that the physical world is a gravitational pull on our consciousness. When our senses are stimulated, the physical world pulls our attention. We interpret the physical world in our habituated way and stay stuck in that interpretation with our mind.

I ask if there is real concrete matter. I am told that as a point of light I am the life force, as is everyone else, which animates matter. I ask if there are physical laws of nature involved that determine parts of our existence. An image of the evolution of a species appears in my mind's eye. I see the changes the species goes through to adapt to a changing environment. I understand that the laws change based upon other factors that are intricately related to the formation of the host environment.

I see clearly how we animate matter, which changes matter, which changes the stimuli that we sense as life, which in turn changes matter. Being part of the process and being aware of the process, observing it, we change the process. Nothing is static, not even the laws of nature. This happens over time, but not really, because time isn't linear, there is only now. We can't perceive the entirety of existence; there is too much stimuli to grasp. Focusing on one thing, we are able to discriminate and be conscious of the present moment.

When we incarnate as humans the physical stimuli overtakes us, and we rely on our senses and mind to interpret our existence. We also rely on our family and cultural beliefs to explain the bombardment of stimuli. Perhaps as we evolve as beings, we will perceive differently, which in turn will change matter, which in turn will change what we sense. A breakthrough in a change in perception could change reality as we currently experience it. The evolution need not be the same slow process if our awareness increases.

Class is over, and I am once again an ordinary woman sitting in her living room on a winter Sunday morning. I grab my journal and start writing before all the mundane activities of my perceived real life take over, and the lessons learned fade from insight to oblivion.

February 2003

I love the Seinfeld episode where George's father's mantra is 'Serenity Now,' and he says the words over and over in anger and frustration. That is me at work, one month after Mexico. I know letting go of judgments is a necessary and prominent theme in Buddhism and the Toltec work I am involved in, but I wonder where clarity leaves off and judgment begins. I chastise myself for judging others, but at times think

I see things more clearly because of the inner work I am doing. I battle between wanting to be compassionate and wanting to run away from the confused ego-driven dramas I run into at work. I bite my tongue, but I am left with unresolved feelings of frustration, since I feel forced to deal with other people's baggage. Did Buddha ever lose it or tell someone to wake up? I know why serious spiritual seekers go on retreat and seek silence. But I need guidance for this situation right here and now.

Luckily the women in Mystica help. They point out that it is my attachment to a certain outcome that is giving me grief. My results oriented approach to life is a habit I must abandon, if I want to release the energy currently tied up in responding to how I think things should be. Rather ironic that this habit has allowed me to accomplish so much in the physical realm but is a deterrent to perceiving other realms of existence. To practice serenity I need to stay focused on the present and release all expectation of a particular outcome. I hope as I release any attachment to results, my natural compassion will slowly return. I hope it happens before I lose it again; I am much closer to love and happiness on the weekends.

One woman on-line shares her awareness of old self-defeating patterns. That part of her e-mail struck a chord with me. Old habits are so insidious! I think I've changed and then something will happen, and I will recognize the beat of an old drum.

Why are humans so habitual? Is it the vestiges of animal instinct? Don't know (as I often say but don't mind admitting anymore.)

I am trying to live each day without expectation or 'setting up.' In other words, pre-living what is to come, so that I can try to control what may happen when I actually get there. Living that way was predictable and flat. But 'setting up' is a habit that has a life of its own. I'm glad I found this path; I am learning to be open to whatever happens and love myself no matter what I feel. Tall order, but I sense progress.

We were supposed to do some soul searching at our first Wisdom Group in 2003 but Joe writes a poem and reads it aloud.

I fly along the top of trees
Soaring over the birds and bees
At this moment I have no weight

My air, my heart, the only freight.
I have no memory of where I was
I'm not even questioning it,
It's just because,
And now I'm not limited to just the sky
I just flew through a mountainside.
Did I change?
Did I just die?
It's peaceful, limitless.
Come with me. Please try.

After reading the poem, the teacher stares at him until he bursts out, "What?"

She tells him, "I'm loving you with my whole heart." And she is.

Soon after the women are separated from the men, and we spend a few hours with gender-specific issues. We discuss body image, and the tendency that many women have to put people and tasks before self-fulfillment.

Near the end of the session, the teacher looks me in the eye and tells me I am a powerful woman. Then she says, "You are a natural; you get it and have great insight. Once you clear the channels and let your emotions be felt, the process and your wisdom will only be enhanced."

Unsure of what the teacher sees in me, her words stick, mixing with a desire to believe what she says, while acknowledging an underlying self-doubt that she has me mistaken for someone else.

Going into the Mitote ritual, I resolve to ask a question about my power. I don't feel powerful most of the time; I am puzzled by the thought of having power but not recognizing it. During my turn at the altar, my personal story doesn't seem to matter. I start from the perspective that I am powerful and ask myself, "What do I want to do with my power?" I breathe deeply as several women advised me to do when I asked them earlier today how to consult my feelings instead of my head. I don't want an answer by thinking about it; I want to feel with my body and let my emotions reveal the answer.

War comes to mind anyway, the brink of war, where we find ourselves yet again. I remember my response to Mystica's email about the impending war with Iraq. This country has a choice: to follow the old path of war or to find a new way out of this conflict and a different way to deal with the fear brought on by terrorism.

I accept that I have no idea how to do this, but I want to lend my powerful intent to finding a new way. Maybe this time we can overcome the old habit of force and instead bring to the negotiating table our common humanity. Find a way that lets everyone benefit from a solution born of mutual respect.

I put my intent out there, wave after wave without forming an illustration of how this would look. My intent is replicated as a mantra for the entire time I am at the altar. My intent is to raise all human souls to the level needed to transcend the past, to change human behavior and create a truly new millennium.

Enjoying the emotions generated by my intent, my spirit is so huge, so expansive that it fills the room. My soul is part of something collective and glorious. My little self is a vehicle, not an obsession, as I shift my attention to the whole of humanity. Cleaning the channels of communication that were blocked with old stories of victimization, allows the soul and heart to focus on the moment; to be present when purpose and compassion intersect and dreams merge and evolution crystallizes in yet another ever changing manifestation of our consciousness. Let compassion color our manifestation. Let love shine through the crystal of every human heart and let it be reflected back a million times over. That is my dream tonight, the dream I throw out to the universe of possibilities.

March 2003

There are only three of us, not including the meditation leader. I can't complain; I almost never make Thursday nights myself. Joy and I kiss when we see each other, but for the life of me, I can't remember the other woman's name. I have seen her here at least twice before. She has a memorable face with unruly orange hair. Maybe that is why I can't remember her name; it is her face that stays with me. No matter, I am here to sit and share mindful conversation, and I don't need a crowd to do it with.

The first meditation is a warm up for me, since I am accustomed to sitting for forty minutes at a time. Walking meditation is not a favorite of mine. The slow steps are relaxing, though, and I am surprised that I walk as slowly as I do. I would go even slower, if I didn't notice the person behind was getting closer while the person in front is walking farther ahead.

At some point I eventually become self-conscious of the lop-sided space in front and behind me, and I quicken my pace to make the line more orderly. Probably not the goal Thich Nhat Hanh had in mind when he practices peace during walking meditations.

The third and last meditation is usually a twenty-minute silent meditation. By the third sitting, my mind is calmer, and I feel the benefits of meditating with a group. I close my eyes and drift in and out of awareness of my slowed but unceasing thoughts. Tonight I have an impression of a more complete darkness than the usual dusky interior of my eyelids. The darkness encases me in a soft blackness, a fur-covered cave for contemplation. I feel another presence with me and peer into the darkness. Opening like thick velvet theatre stage curtains, the soft blackness parts — and an ugly green gremlin steps into view.

Shocked by the hideous looking creature, I recoil from the vision unfolding before me. The gremlin only stands there, and I realize the apparition won't hurt me. Far from fierce, the creature looks sad and lonely. Feeling the pain coming from the poor creature's shame and hesitancy, I recognize the repulsive green creature as me. I know the gremlin to be all the things I hate about myself. I know how much this part of me has suffered because of my self-hatred. I open my arms and the gremlin comes toward me. I cradle its ugly hairless body as I would a small child. I open my heart more, and the gremlin fits perfectly into the folds of my body as I rock slightly back and forth. I comfort my little gremlin and feel a peace descend over me that I have not felt since Teotihuacan.

The meditation bowl is chimed. The session is over. But I cannot easily come out of the trance I entered when the soft blackness enveloped me.

The meditation teacher is looking at me and asks us to share. Joy and the orange haired woman say a few words about the war, and when they are done the teacher turns to me and says, "Something happened, didn't it?"

My mouth won't move and let any words out. I do not tell them what happened, but manage to say I am glad I can be amongst peaceful people at this violent time in our country. As if in slow motion the words take a long time to form in my head and even longer to physically come out of my lips. The gremlin and the soft cave space I have been in seem more authentic than the present environment in which I am being asked to participate. I don't know why I don't tell the truth, and the teacher looks at me, as if she expects more, but the effort to speak is too much — and I fall silent.

A week after discovering my neglected self, I give my first non-summer service. That means speaking in front of a full house. My service is inspired by our trip to France. I ask the congregation to imagine what life may have been like if Unitarian Universalism had been the dominant religion instead of the Roman Catholic Church during the Middle Ages. Imagine tolerance instead of oppressive domination. Imagine men and women equal partners in worship. Imagine openness instead of inquisitions — Agape feasts instead of religious crusades.

Of course, Universalist Universalism might not have come into being if the dominant religions of the past hadn't perpetuated oppressive dogmas of intolerance, insecurity and fear. The need for a faith in universal salvation would not have existed. I end our worship hour together with a reading and response of the seven guiding principles of Unitarian Universalism.

The inherent worth and dignity of every person.

Justice, equity, and compassion in human relations.

Acceptance of one another and encouragement to spiritual growth in our congregations.

A free and responsible search for truth and meaning.

The right of conscience and the use of the democratic process within our congregations and in the society at large.

The goal of world community with peace, liberty and justice for all.

Respect for the interdependent web of all existence of which we are a part.

April 2003

I'm asked to post *Karyn's No Spoon Theory* for Mystica when I told the meditation leader about the incident. The e-mail is long, but I wanted the contents to be coherent. The 'No-Spoon' theory is an explanation of a teaching I received in a dream a few nights ago. I add a background to the teaching, since the movie instigated the dream. With a click on the send button, I share my first teaching.

At a recent Wisdom Group gathering, the teacher asked us to watch *The Matrix*. Most of us had seen the movie at least once, but she wanted us to watch it again with the recent lessons in mind. In one scene of the movie Neo, the main character, is waiting to see the oracle. There is a child holding a spoon, and he is bending the spoon with his mind. Neo watches, and the child says to Neo, "There is no spoon." Then I think the child says, "You bend."

That part of the movie stayed with me for days. The "there is no spoon" statement resonated deeply with me, but I didn't understand what it meant to me in reference to the lessons.

Shortly after watching the movie, I had a dream, a teaching dream. So much so, that I woke up after the teaching and wrote it down in the middle of the night. The dream was mostly visual, and must have had some words also, but none I can directly quote. The teaching was about the nature of reality and why there is no spoon.

The mind, like a computer, is capable of very complex tasks. But if you get down to the most basic computer programming, down to its core, machine language, there are only zeros and ones in infinite combinations. All computer programs come down to this. All the programs layered on top of the machine language are merely there to allow humans to program and interact with the computer's processing chip. Ultimately the computer is only processing two things, zero or one.

The mind is very complex but relies on the brain as a physical organ. The brain operates with chemical reactions and tiny electronic impulses. While we are awake, the mind will focus on a small portion of a vast amount of stimuli. After the mind focuses, puts attention on an event taking place outside of the mind, the brain processes the incoming stimulus. Essentially at the core of the processing, the brain is either giving the incoming stimulus a light on (thumbs up) or light off (thumbs down), depending on how the mind perceives the event. The perception is based on the past, since the mind has to relate the incident to something already experienced. The event is really made up of many tiny quick perceptions that get processed by the brain: light on, light off.

The elemental brain was pictured as a long pole with small floodlights covering its entire length. When stimuli are perceived by the mind and passed onto the brain, the lights go on or off. A perception associated with a positive memory, a floodlight clicks on. A perception associated with a past negative experience, a light will go off. The lights are constantly flickering on and off as the brain processes events as perceptions based on past experience. Any given event that is focused on, results in many lights being either on or off. If more lights are off, the judgment and resulting interpretation of the emotion associated with the current event is interpreted as 'bad,' even though the association made by the mind is based on a past experience. That is the only way an association can be made by the mind. If more lights are on, then an overall interpretation and judgment of 'good' results.

This goes on constantly as the day is lived. On, off, on off. There is no reality or solid beginning or ending to an event. There is only the perception and interpretation of whatever we happen to be giving our attention to at that moment. This accounts for differing interpretations of events, likes and dislikes among people, cultures, and countries. People focus on different stimulus, filter their perceptions with different past experiences and cultural interpretations. But each individual brain processes very basically, light on, light off. There is no spoon, only perception and interpretation of fleeting feelings rekindled from the past.

What changes with our awareness of this process is detachment. We can detach from our response to an event. Since the perception is essentially based on the past, the feeling associated with the incident doesn't mean much. Light on, light off, big deal. We can now choose to interpret whatever we think we have experienced because we are aware of the on-off switch. We can choose the emotional result of the experience once we detach from the habitual reaction. We may still have uncomfortable feelings; but we don't need to get caught up with them, unless we want to investigate the past.

Since the dream, when I find myself interpreting an event negatively because I feel 'bad,' I conjure up the image of myself as a walking blinking set of lights. I can't help but to immediately let go of the judgment and interpretation because of the absurdity of the image. I realize it is a process, not the event, which is leading to the judgment. We react emotionally to the events we encounter during the day. We believe it is reality we are experiencing, but we aren't. We are experiencing an interpretation of an internal process. There is no spoon.

These concepts are reinforced by my experience with night dreaming. I have gone from being awake straight into a dream. There is no 'asleep' in between. Both states — awake and dream — feel equally real in the moment my brain/body experiences them. My brain is processing both states exactly the same way whether the stimulus comes from my five senses or my subconscious. Lights on, lights off — same process, same illusion of reality.

You might say, "Yes, but one state is real, and one is a dream!"

No, one has a denser framework, but how I experience both of them is the same. My perception and interpretation, and, therefore, my experience of reality aren't dependent on any outside event. Reality is an internal process.

The meditation leader writes back after I send 'The No Spoon theory." She explains how even the 0 and 1 is further broken down to a scale of 1 through 10. There is a threshold of activity that needs to be measured for a 1 or 0 value to be returned to the computer's processor. Only the ends of the scale, the extremes, register enough to result in a signal of 0 or 1 to a computer. If we use the analogy with the brain again, this means we are only experiencing the extremes of existence. The events that happen that don't make the threshold are below our awareness. Doing internal spiritual work could mean we can become aware of the activity that doesn't normally make it over the threshold — the gray, mystical, intuitive episodes. Which leads me to another's e-mail response: the more we sensitize to the finer energy fields, the more we will be able to bend reality or use the energy matrix more artfully.

Receiving feedback on my theory is satisfying and I enjoy sharing my teaching almost as much as giving a Service on Sunday with my fellowship.

* * *

I had a run-in with my new client this week.

She is going through some personal problems and decided to take it out on me. She insinuated that I was wasting time on a new project. She used a condescending and derisive tone of voice while questioning me about the work I had done so far.

I became upset and took a walk and decided I had to confront her with my feelings. I went to her office, and we barely avoided an emotional confrontation as I held my ground and refused to sell myself short because she appeared to hold the power position.

My client tried to rationalize her behavior again by pointing out what she thought I had done, but I knew she was reacting out of her own suffering. I was not the only person she had targeted with her deflected disappointment and anger.

I told her I treat her with a great deal of respect, and I want the same in return. I wrote a memo the next day to her and her boss, explaining my position, and I advised them to look for another person to take on the project if they were unhappy or cost was an issue.

"There must have been a miscommunication," her boss said.

And I agreed.

If I give myself the compassion and support I believe everyone else deserves, then truly no one can hurt me. I am protected by my own love, which is so much healthier than my old childhood defenses of rationalization and denial.

Beauty is
before me

THE A-FRAME LIVING ROOM IS DECORATED IN A STYLE REMINISCENT OF THE 70S. I sit cross-legged on the sofa with two other women, while the others in the semi-dark room sit likewise on the multi-colored shag carpet. Our teacher is leading the morning meditation. She speaks of rising to a higher, clearer space. She instructs us to connect with the group, to go beyond the thinking mind and reach out for the clear space. I don't know what she is talking about. I usually meditate alone, and I never truly understand what is meant by 'clear space.' I only know to watch my thoughts and let them go, to not go off on a tangent and become entangled in my little cognition creations.

Connect with the group; now I worry about connecting with the group. Let's see, there is the wizard, my secret title for the tall, authoritative woman sitting beside me; the disillusioned ex- nun, a spiritual being with no home; a sweet voiced single mom is sitting on my left and an extremely funny, self-deprecating therapist is in the corner. There is the artist and the gladiator woman with a heart of gold to my right. And then, of course, facing the rest of us is Gayle, the meditation teacher turned Mystery School headmistress.

Connect with them — I don't even know why I'm here — here in Lafollette, Tennessee, sharing a three-bedroom summer cottage with seven women for seven days. I have met only one of the women before, and that was a brief but amazing meeting. I know them only through the e-mails we have been exchanging since last fall; we are Mystica.

119

I decide to forget about the connecting business, go back to the basics and follow my breath. Breathe in, breathe out, breathe in, and breathe out. After a few moments of watching my breath, I notice a soft, bright white illumination settle around me. This is unusual; I usually am in the dark when I meditate.

Looking straight ahead, I see myself sitting on a swing — the kind of swing you would find hanging from a large tree in the country. Only this swing is not attached to a tree or anything at all. Nonetheless, I am able to swing back and forth. The soft, white bright light creates a halo around me. The edge of the light dissolves into blackness. There is nothing else in the vision.

Swinging slowly in the light, I notice my hair lifting up as I swing down, as if the air current is holding my limp curls up. I watch, fascinated as my hair falls back onto my head, before I pump myself forward and skyward. I am curious about my hair; why is such a detail there? Focusing in, I imagine the air gently moving across my face — when I see my hair swing out and away from my head. Why am I noticing?

"To know there is wind," pops into my head. Of course! I think, the sensation of wind is attainable once I see my hair moving in it. I know the wind exists in the vision, since I can see the movement of my hair.

"Why are we here?" I ask, though I didn't know I had a question.

"To know there is God," comes the answer.

Of course! Someone has to observe the miracle of existence for existence to be known. We are here to let God know God exists! It seems so obvious, clear and distinctly true. I rest in a contented, gentle state, until the vision passes; then I wait for the Tibetan bells to end the meditation. In less than a month's time, I will find writings attributable to Annie Dillard in my hymnal that expresses my vision flawlessly.

We are here to abet creation and to give witness to it, to notice each other's beautiful face and complex nature so that creation need not play to an empty house.

In the afternoon following my morning vision, the former nun applies plaster-soaked gauze strips to my face that's heavy with Vaseline. Her fingers are ever so gentle as she presses gauze strips onto my skin, so that they won't slip when the next layer is applied. The process is slow and intimate as the strips go over my lips. I keep my eyes closed, though no gauze covers them. Masks traditionally have eyeholes for the wearer to see through. I'm grateful for that; the plaster is starting to harden, and I am claustrophobic already.

All too soon my face is immobilized. I can't smile, raise my eyebrows or wrinkle my nose. The immobile face gives rise to a sensation of general immobility. I am a statue, fixed and frozen in time. My breathing slows as I go further into the granite impressions taking over my body and mind. As my breathing and mind retreat, I am aware of being exquisitely present for each moment, and time is slowing down. The more I notice my static body and face, the more I perceive myself as not being part of this fixed entity. I am not fixed to what I perceive as not moving. I feel fluid while my body feels static. I am not this body. I am something else, something more expansive. I hear a voice from far away ask if I'm ok, but I can't answer; my lips are frozen in the hard mummy gauze.

Days later, sitting on the couch again, meditating with Mystica is easier. I don't worry if I'm missing something or doing it wrong. I relax into the silence of the sitting. I can't help wonder for a moment why the other women often describe visions of mystical places or mythological symbols while meditating.

As I let that thought go, I make room to receive the message:

"*Symbols are divisive, light is universal.*"

And again the soft, yet bright white light descends like a misty cloud around me. Dark no more, my meditative space is in the midst of a white light that resembles fog, more than blinding white light — foggy, not because it is hard to see, but because the light is not solid. I see black spaces in between the light, especially around the edges where the light fades into the black.

I feel comfortable and peaceful, sitting silently in the light. After a few minutes, I remember the first time a similar message came into my full awareness. A service was given by a young middle-eastern woman who worked for an organization that tried to get Palestinian and Jewish settlers together to discuss their situation. Her organization's hope was — as each side listened to the other — the warring fractions would find a common experience to bring them closer to what they shared. At the same time, people would have a chance to hear each other's stories and acknowledge each other's humanity.

She was passionate and articulate, and I had the sense that her heart and soul were behind her work. She wore a large Jewish Star of David on a long chain around her neck. I wondered, as I listened to the heartfelt presentation of her group's work, how Palestinian villagers would react to her approaching them, wearing that particular necklace. She used the term, "Holy Land," and explained how the word meant one thing to a group of people and something else to another group; and as a result, how the struggle to share the Holy Land was fraught with centuries of bitter acrimony and death. I asked her what her organization was doing about the symbols that have become embedded with meanings, those symbols that continue to reinforce the differences among the various groups. Was there any thought to creating new symbols that represented the Palestinians, Jews and Christians together?

I was hoping my question would give her pause to reflect on her own choice of symbols. Unitarian Universalists have congregants from all backgrounds: Catholic, Muslim, Jewish, Protestant, Buddhist and even Agnostics. Wearing such a large piece, I assume she identifies with the symbol strongly. Without uttering a word, and before we know anything else about her or the wonderful work she is engaged in, she has aligned herself with a complete ideology and thousands of years of history.

I do not think she understands the question; she uses the term, "Holy Land," again in her attempt to explain the history of the conflict. I was unable to give up my idea that something fundamental was being assumed about the whole Mid-East in this conversation. I decided to be blasphemous in my next statement to her. "You keep referring to the Holy Land. It is no more holy than my backyard. You speak of land that various parties have decided to fight and die over. But its Holiness is due to human belief by the warring parties involved, not to any physical or spiritual trait evident on this particular piece of real estate."

She is taken aback and replied that real events had taken place there. Abraham, David and Jesus had been there; the land had undergone centuries of struggle and conquest.

"Yes," I said, "but that doesn't mean it is anything other than land, unless a person chooses to endow some special meaning to the place. I can do the same to a few feet in my backyard. The history doesn't have to drive the present. Referring to area in conflict as the Holy Land is a symbolic choice of words. Doing so keeps alive the message that the land is worth owning, occupying, fighting and dying for."

I wonder if the land was referred to as 'a rocky desert that needs tremendous effort to be livable' instead of 'The Holy Land;' under these circumstances, people might have realized there was more to gain by cooperation than fighting.

Our choice of words and symbols helps to continue divisiveness among people who have no earthly reason to fight each other and everything to gain by cooperation. Our physical reality does not cause most of our wars. The interpretation of the Divine is what is divisive. Access to the Divine is open to all. To parse divinity further is to invite hell on earth. Which is what has happened. Maybe it is time to ditch all the symbols and start with something inclusive and universally shared. Light is universal, as is access to the Divine. The message in my meditation is simple. Truth, once understood, always is.

In the evening we watch *The Journey of Man*, a PBS special about tracing human DNA roots to a single village in Africa. The documentary asserts that as few as ten people migrating over the Bering Straight could have populated all of North America. Adam and Eve meets Stanford University genetics lab. They seem to be telling similar stories.

Two days later for twenty-five bucks I am on the earlier, direct flight from Knoxsville to LaGuardia. Soooo much better than having a layover. I have been gone seven days, the longest I have ever been away by myself. I am anxious to see my family and sleep in my own bed.

I have a window seat with no one next to me and stretch out. Outside the window are deep white canyons and spiraling mountains. Big fat fluffy marshmallow clouds up close, almost touchable. The sun bounces off the silvery fissures creating endless hues of gold and pink. The outer limits of the sky high landscape are wispy cotton candy. The underside is dark gray, pregnant with rain. Tiny droplets of water decorate the oval shaped airplane window and I visualize the act of condensation taking place as the dense cloud molecules become heavy, transforming into water. The creation of a single drop of rain, each luminous bulb falls to earth alone, like a solitary soul being born human. I wonder if we are one huge dynamic essence and the flowing act of creation causes us to fall off separately to earth, living and then dying, then transforming once again from flesh to spirit; like water to vapor, reuniting into one again, like the clouds in the heavens.

Looking away from the window, I decide to let a recommended book from the retreat open to any page. The book falls open to *Becoming the Lotus*. The passage is as perfect for the moment as the heavens outside my window.

> *I open and light descends, fills me and passes through, each thin blue petal reflected perfectly in clear water. I am that lotus filled with light reflected perfectly in clear water. I am that lotus filled with light reflected in the world. I float content within myself, one flower with a thousand petals, one life lived a thousand years without haste, one universe sparking a thousand stars, one god alive in a thousand people.*[2]

May 2003

When I return to work I tape the letters GFD on a yellow post it note to the lower right hand corner of my computer monitor. There, if I see the note enough, maybe I will remember to follow the instructions. Gap, Feel, Detach. The therapist from my Mystica retreat filled in the missing component of my Gap and Detach maneuver. She told me I have to feel before I detach.

I had been confused in Tennessee as to how I was supposed to refrain from responding habitually to someone and detaching without suppressing some emotional response. I mean, that is the whole point, isn't it? Not to respond emotionally and irrationally and create the same poisonous action-reaction in situations that make me crazy. Detachment is a mechanism for not letting my buttons get pushed, isn't it? Even practicing the gap and detaching, the emotion gets stuck, stuck inside my body, my clenched teeth, and my churning stomach.

"Feel it first, then let it go," I was told when I asked how not to suppress an emotion from which I want to detach myself. Allow for a Gap, a slight pause before reacting. Feel. Allow the emotion to come up whether it is anger, shame, fear or whatever. Detach, let the feeling flow through and let it go after it is acknowledged and physically felt by the body. Feel the emotion without reacting or taking action. "G F D. Gap, Feel, Detach," I said out loud.

"Yup, it's a Good Fucking Deal," retorted the therapist.

And that is how I remember it.

After following Dr Phil's *Self Matters* exercises as advised by the headmistress, I decide to see my psychologist friend again. I accept now that being abandoned at age two probably was a big deal. I don't want the issue to be working behind the scenes in my current relationships, and I need help figuring it all out.

The night before my third appointment with my therapist, I have a dream. I am at the airport waiting to board my plane. I am waiting outside on the tarmac with a man I know from the Wisdom Group. A baggage cart comes along and picks up our luggage and starts to leave. We realize that the baggage cart is the only way to get to the plane, and he is able to jump onto the cart as it pulls away. I don't move fast enough and am left standing on the tarmac all alone. I look at the people on the baggage cart and see Joe. He looks at me and shrugs his shoulders, an expression that says ooops sorry, nothing I can do. I see my friend turn around and glance at me, before settling into a seat on the baggage cart turned Disney tram.

I understand that I will not make the plane and that Joe and my friend are not going to help me. I open my mouth and scream, loud and long. The sound I make is a baby's scream. I scream so loud the whole airport can hear me. I wake up with my mouth, if not my eyes, wide open.

Now
I recall
my childhood

Spoke to my mother on the phone today. Asked her how the barbeque at the minister's new house went. Her reply clarified the source of my deepest conflict in life. "Very nice. You know when you don't have kids you can have a library and den with the extra rooms." A pause on the other end of the line, then she personalizes what she has just said with, "Not that I would ever not want to have had you kids."

My mother told me she loved me when I was growing up, but, oh, what a burden was the adjacent, unspoken statement. To be loved and cared for costs the person loving you. This viewpoint conveyed by my mother in so many off-hand remarks stems from an event that happened early in my life; an event that would shape my early childhood development; an event that I wouldn't know the truth about until I was forty. There are still aspects of what happened that I will never know; aspects that my mother won't examine today. Such is the power of denial and the resiliency of protecting our self-image.

I was two years old, sitting in the back seat of an automobile. My brother Eric, who is a year younger, is sitting next to me. The seat is big and roomy, and I can't see much over the front seat that is directly in front of me. The windows are open, but we are not moving. I hear my mother, who had been driving the car, get out and start talking to a man at the gas station. After a moment the car begins to move forward. Something is not right, though. There is nobody in the front seat.

The car starts rolling down a hill, faster and faster. Crying, I stand up on the floor to look over the front seat and out the windshield. I see the steep hill we are speeding down and the cars we are going to crash into at the bottom. I can't stop the car. I don't know how to stop the car! I don't understand why no one stops the car.

Where is my mommy? Where is my daddy?

I scream, "Help us! Help us! Help me!"

The traffic in the cross street is in front of me. The car is not going to stop; no one is going to save me. I am going to die.

I gasp for air, my body stiff with anticipation of an enormous impact with metal and death. Just as the car I am riding in is about to crash I reach out my arms to brace myself and my mind wrenches me from the terrible scene — and suddenly I am awake. Instead of unyielding steel, I feel the soft mattress of my bed underneath my back.

I always wake up on my back a split second before the crash. Always convinced of my certain death — until the moment I wake up. The nightmare is all too familiar. I dream it repeatedly from the time I can remember until I am eleven years old. I can't remember most of the event that shaped my childhood, maybe because I was only two at the time. One small memory and the reoccurring nightmare are proof enough of the event's impact on my life.

Growing up, I had been told only a part of the story that was the source of this recurring nightmare, the part where my mother is fiercely devoted to her children. The part of the story that wasn't told for almost forty years, holds the key that would shape not only my nightmares but would help create an anxiety that underscores many of the adult relationships in my life.

In fairness to my mother I have to tell the story with a bit of background. Nothing happens in a vacuum, and I shouldn't judge her until I have walked a mile in her shoes and even then, judging does no good, only harm. I did judge my mother when I found out the truth. I still work on not judging my parents, wishing things had been different. I have to remind myself that they gave me more then they had emotionally and materially. Most days I can let my disappointment go. But for two years I could barely speak to my mother. I resented those years growing up, thinking that my brothers and I were to blame somehow, reminded by my father when my mother was depressed or irritable that she is vulnerable, and we should behave in case she dissolves in nervous agony again. I believed we were too burdensome for an emotionally fragile woman like my mother. Guilt, deserved or not, hangs heavy on a child.

My father worked six, sometimes seven days a week. As a chef, he worked fourteen-hour days, covering both lunch and dinner. As customary in the restaurant business, he drank a lot. No one said the word alcoholic in those days, but that is what he was. He was verbally and sometimes physically abusive to my mother. The marriage was in trouble by the time my brother Brian was born. He was the second child and second boy. By the time my younger brother Eric was born, child number four, my mother was, as she often reminded us, ready to put her head in the oven.

When I was two and Eric one, my mother left my father and took her children to stay with her uncle. After a few weeks away from home, she decided to patch things up with my father.

On the night before she is to return home to her husband, she goes out with a friend to a local tavern. She meets and falls in love with a younger man who works at a gas station. They have an affair, and she decides she no longer wants to be married to my father. She wants to be with the man she has just met and loves.

Even though she decides to be with the new lover, she returns with her children to the apartment she shares with my father. While there, she waits for her lover to call and come for her. As she waits and he does not call, she loses twenty pounds because she cannot eat or sleep. At some point my father confronts my mother with her odd behavior, and she confesses to the affair. Not only does she confess, she lets my father know how much she loves this new man. My father nearly chokes her to death. The next thing my mother remembers is being committed to a private mental institution by my father because of an apparent nervous breakdown.

After six weeks of hospitalization, my mother refuses to return to my father and in retaliation my father has her committed to a state mental institution. My mother's deaf mother, who has been taking care of us while Mommy is in a hospital, refuses to care for us any longer unless my father signs the papers to get my mother out. Grandma was hoping this would dissuade my father from actually committing her daughter to a state insane asylum. It does not deter my father, and my brothers go into foster care. I am given to family friends for safekeeping. I am two, and I will not see my family again for a year.

As the family story goes, nine months after my mother's oldest sister gets my mother out of the mental institution, my grandmother and aunt decide they should get the children out of foster care and reunite us with our mother. They consult a lawyer and a clergyman. They are given the advice not to go to court; custody could be a problem with my mother's institutionalization. Better to gather the kids and start from there. Possession is nine-tenths of the law, whether you are a child or piece of property. So one day, after living with my new family for a year, one third of my little life, my mother shows up and asks to take me to lunch. My new mother, who has taken me in as one of her own, does not want to say no, and she lets me go with my mother. I do not see my second family again for thirty-six years.

By the time I was four I had lost two mothers and been returned to one, a volatile one. Ironically my mother returned to my father when I was six and became pregnant with my sister Kim, her fifth and final child. My mother will repeat the same scenario when I am eleven — different lover, same mental institution. We are old enough and are able to watch my baby sister, avoiding foster care this time around. When I am twelve, my parents divorce, and the Greek tragedy that was their marriage finally ends.

My mother's recounting puts her in the hero's seat. She has to overcome all obstacles to snatch her children back and reunite the family under one roof. It wasn't until I had my own child and he turned two that I began to question the story. I realized that my mother kidnapping me back was as traumatic as losing her in the first place.

The story told to everyone else for thirty-seven years did not reveal a lover. No one knew why my father choked my mother. When I asked my mother why her lover never called or came to get her she says she imagines he didn't want a woman with four kids. Her impersonal resentment of her children as obstacles to what might have been, acknowledged by her or not, is an undercurrent in our relationship until she retires and comes to live with Joe and me.

I never would have discovered any of the extenuating details except I went to a therapist at age forty to figure out why I had trouble being civil to my mother while she lived in my house. The story always had holes, but I never had the courage to question my mother until my therapist pointed out that, as a child, my feelings were never mentioned or considered, not even by me.

Existence
is beyond
the power
of words
to define

THE SECOND DREAM IN NEW JERSEY IS THE INSPIRATION FOR TODAY'S SERVICE.
The vision of cups running over with golden liquefied light moves
me to find a way to share my thoughts on giving and receiving.
I have noticed that the people who care the most about social
justice often appear drained of energy from the weight of those
concerns. Not always, but enough that the syndrome makes me
leery. One of the reasons I choose Unitarian Universalism as my
religion is because the faith is involved in creating social justice.
I don't want a serving of guilt along with the creation. Motivation
for helping others or visioning a kinder world doesn't come from
a sense of duty as far as I am concerned. No, service to others
comes from a cup that runneth over.

I uncover supporting words in favorite books and read excerpts
to support my view during the service. I hope those weary from
tasks of the heart listen and give themselves the opportunity to fill
up before taking on the world again. The Chalice lighting begins
with words from Dag Hammarskjold.

*Each morning we must hold out the chalice of our being
to receive, to carry, and give back.*

131

June 2003

One of the themes this weekend is obstacles to love and living in love. After twenty-four hours of contemplation I come to the conclusion that my biggest obstacle to love is not being able to love myself at any given moment. I love myself conditionally. There is usually some standard or measurement I must meet to feel good about myself. To love myself is an obstacle because I know self-love precedes non-judgment and acceptance of what is, which precedes loving all and being in love with life. I understand I will have to find a way to accept and love myself at every moment, regardless of where I am in reaching my goals. Accept myself whether I am feeling good about a relationship or not. Accept my emotions no matter what form they take.

Saturday night is my first mirror Mitote, an all night meditation where people take turns looking in a mirror in the candlelight. I want to look in the mirror and see if I can accept myself as I am. Can I be there with myself and feel love for myself without judgment or accomplishment? My reflection is a surprise. There is no animation. If I stare and do not blink, my eyes look painted on, as if I were an Egyptian mummy. That is a container, not a person before me. I realize that it isn't me in the mirror, only a vessel. I am alive, but what is in the mirror is not me. I am life, and I can not be contained by a body.

After my turn at the mirror I hear an apprentice of Don Miguel remind us that "All you have to do is remember that you are dreaming." With a sleepless yawn I draw my knees to my chest and let my heavy head sink as low as my exhausted neck allows. I surrender my head to my heart and breathe deeply into the small space between my knees and chest. Soon after, I have a vision. I am walking on a small grassy hill in the distance. While walking, I pick 'stuff' out of the air. My arms raise over my head as I pinch a bit of this and that from the darkness surrounding me. The nothing surrounding me I know to be the void. I am gathering bits and pieces out of nothing and creating. I understand that I am life, creating life, out of the void. I pause and contemplate my creation and decide I don't like it. I wave my hand and, it is erased, gone. It is a dream, my life dream — to create and re-create at will.

The vision dissipates as casually as my creation from the void. A different realm of consciousness overtakes me, and I am back in a candlelit room, wanting everyone in the world to know that they are creators; that they don't need to live up to anyone else's version of themselves.

When sharing my experience the next day the teacher tells me, "You are dreaming you! And if everyone knew that, what kind of world would this be?"

Indeed, what kind of world? How would we dream ourselves, if we realized we are our own creation?

The last weekend in June, I attend a new healers' support group. I came to be supportive of my friend the Reiki master from the Wisdom weekends. I had one incredible experience in a faith healing workshop, but am ambivalent about energy healing. Touchy-feely to the extreme; I'm glad the field is gaining credibility but don't see myself engaging further in the practice.

Sunday morning a faith healer leads the healing circle in a meditation and asks us to go deep and hold the space while she calls us up separately to kneel in front of her. When I kneel in front of her chair I am told to surrender, and I lower my head. I am told to surrender again and then again, until my head is in her lap. I am told to let go of my old life, to forget my past, clean my lineage and break away from its patterns.

I am told I will give birth but not physically. I will give birth to myself; I will be reborn. I am told that my way is to write a book, and I am being given a golden plume in my hand with which to write the book. I will receive the Divine messages, and they will come out of my lips with authority and conviction. I am told that my writing will make people understand; they will read my words and experience my visions. I am told to continue my work clearing myself of old habits and attachments, so that I can become a clearer mirror for everyone. I am to take the cotton ball with the oil and put it in a red pouch and place the pouch in the room where I will be working, the new room that is being prepared for me by me. I am told that my spiritual guide for the rest of this life is Isaiah, and he will provide inspiration and guidance for my book.

Astounded, I lift my head, look straight into the healer's eyes, and she says, "Remember — you are pregnant! In nine months, you will be reborn."

I move back to my seat on the couch and look over at her while she channels for the last person in the group. Her long, straight blond hair is tucked behind her ears. Her blue eyes are crystal clear as she relays her message to the woman kneeling before her. Twenty-something, she looks like she came straight off a California beach. Looks aside, she is the clearest person I have come across since Don Miguel. I guess being Don Miguel's mother's successor is a cleansing process in itself. The healer has been working as Mother Sarita's apprentice for three years and is Sarita's handpicked successor. She told me they dreamed of each other before they actually met — the young woman is from New England, Mother Sarita is from Mexico.

How the hell did she know about the book? Or the room? Only Joe and the boys know about my desire to write a book, and I have almost talked myself out of it. Writing the book seems impractical, a long shot, not something I am capable of. The room spoken of is the upstairs kitchen that Joe and I are converting into a meditation/sunroom. The room came in a vision to me on the subway one day almost two years ago. I finally told Joe about my idea for the room, and he agreed. We had just hired someone to replace the old windows with five-foot high wall-to-wall windows so the room will be flooded with light.

The healer tells us she doesn't remember what she says, that she channels energy moving through her. I ask her about Isaiah anyway; but she knows even less then me. I at least know he was a prophet in the Old Testament. Not that that excites me. The Bible has never been my favorite book.

July 2003

Whoever created Amazon.com knows what they are doing. I want to order one book and end up buying three. This time the advertisement "other people who ordered *Instinct for Freedom* also ordered *The Power of Now* by Eckhart Tolle" keeps popping up. The effective sales pitch must have popped up three times in a row; finally I click on Add to Cart. Glad I did. It is probably the clearest spiritual book I have ever read.

Tolle doesn't talk in circles, defining a concept using the same word within the definition. He explains the non-rational in practical terms. I have referred to myself as 'practical pig' on more than one occasion, as opposed to practical pig's brothers, who built their houses with straw and sticks. No one in my family has ever accused me of being fanciful.

None of the Buddhist books explained so pragmatically the rewards of living in the now. Tolle gives numerous practical examples on how to accomplish the feat. Not that it is an easy thing to do; like everything else; living in the now is a choice, a conscious choice. I want to remember so much in the book, but I settle for the one thing I can pull out easily and what helps me the most.

When I start to cycle around a perceived problem I ask myself, "Is it a problem now?" I actually hear the guy on the Sprint commercial in my head, "Can you hear me now?" What a brilliant commercial. I change the words to, "Is it a problem now?" I find that unless I am going to be hit by a bus in the next second, the answer is invariably, "No." At this exact moment, it is not a problem. It may become one, if I ignore it, but right this second there is no need to panic, no fight or flight response is called for. I have no reason for obsession. If there is a need for possible action in the future, I write it down. Then I let it go, along with the discordant emotion that inevitably accompanies my internally created problems. Whew! What a relief the question brings. Look at the situation for what it is and let it go. So much energy freed up and available; for the moment I am alive in, right now. What a pile of mind clutter is thrown out with that simple question, "Is it a problem now?"

The sky is a clear, clean blue with wispy clouds forming on the horizon. The sun is hot, without burning, on my skin while the pool water cools the lower part of my body. I am supported by a floating foam chair that is currently equipped with a bowl of cherries and a glass of Syrah wine. I hear my son's voice coming from the neighbor's pool a few houses away. Sounds of Marco . . .Polo . . . Marco . . . Polo drifts over to my yard on the breezy balmy air that belongs to this perfect summer day.

What a peaceful, satisfying moment. How good is this moment with everything calm, gentle and enjoyable. But I know all is not well in the world. I have been reading Alan Clements's *Instinct for Freedom* and wonder how I can be so blissful when I am connected to all the suffering in the world.

"*It goes both ways,*" I am told by a thought that descends like a message from someone outside of me. I recognize that my bliss is also part of the world community and consciousness. The connection to everyone goes both ways. I am not separate, and my bliss can also calm the cosmic human consciousness, just as the suffering of my fellow humans creates fear and angst for me. I need not constantly be attuned only to my sisters and brothers suffering, I can allow others to wallow in my bliss. I wish the world could join me in my pool and share my wine and cherries. I accept what is right now and try not to make a problem for myself when clearly, at this moment, there isn't one.

The boat rocks furiously from the waves pounding against the windows that enclose the inside of the commercial fishing boat. I ask the captain if we are going to be all right. He says the storm isn't that bad, that we will get through. I turn my head slightly to look past his reassuring face and see a wall of water right in front of the boat. "Holy shit!" I yell as I brace myself against the handrail attached to the side of the cabin wall. I hold my breath as the wave hits, and we are smothered under water. Panic sweeps over me as I know I can't hold my breath forever, trapped in this underwater grave.

Turning my head I see Garrett and Andrew, dry and relaxed sitting with dangling legs on a nearby fence. I ask them how this is possible and they tell me they left the boat before the wave hit. "How did you do that?" I ask.

"We just left," they say.

By the time I wake up, my neck is stiff. By the end of the day I can barely move my head to the right; the muscles in my shoulders are rock solid and in spasm.

My body believes the wave actually hit me. Holding my breath sure didn't help. Damn, why didn't those ungrateful kids take me off the boat with them? Four days of pain and two chiropractic visits later, my neck and shoulders finally relax into their normal positions.

The wave shows up again, this time in meditation. There is a wave of energy coming at me from left to right. I do not hold my breath, remembering the last wave and how I braced for impact. This time, I let the wave pass through me. I visualize myself expanding and allow more space between my cells. The wave of energy moves through me as I stay loose and semi-transparent. I imagine this is how to manage a shift, a change or a catastrophe. Unless, of course, you can do what my kids did and simply get out of the way.

* * *

All the molecules in my body vibrate like microscopic beads suspended in front of a surround sound stereo speaker. They come together by an unseen force and slowly solidify as I become conscious. I don't know who or what I am at the moment, but am spellbound by the electrical juice pulsating through the flesh that is coming alive. Feeling myself become real, almost thirty seconds pass before I realize I am lying on a cot in a tent cabin in the woods at Omega. Joe and I are here for Deepak Chopra's *How to Know God* workshop. I remember my decapitation dream, the re-animation ending. I am definitely awake. I was sleeping. I don't remember any dreams before waking. Waking up is phenomenal enough. My soul has re-entered my dense physical body.

Now fully awake, I indulge my imagination and wonder if my experience is what it would feel like if Scotty really could beam-up Captain Kirk on the Enterprise. Except this is not TV, this is me — me being somewhere else and coming back here. If a transporter ever were created, I imagine, the device would only transport physical cells. The soul is non-local, unconfined to a specific place or time, according to Deepak. The soul can go from here to there instantly. No transporter needed for the soul. But what is a body without a soul? Dead meat, I guess, given the experience I just had.

I listen to the night sounds in the woods. I listen to Joe's even breath coming from the cot three feet away. They aren't joking when they say the workshops are experiential at Omega. And then, thankfully, I drift off back to sleep.

Oddly enough, Deepak mentions moments of non-identity before waking the next day. The synchronicity encourages me to question him during a break about my nightly reentry. We talk of dream yoga, and I promise to forward him a website link when I get home.

The topic turns to karma in the afternoon. Deepak talks as if there is no question that karma exists and is a powerful force in our lives. I'm not totally convinced by his arguments, but I did encounter something like instant karma one day years ago on the highway.

The weather was much like it is now, blue, clear skies accompanied with a sense of clarity that brings high expectations for the day. I was driving my first car equipped with carpeting and air conditioning.

My brother Brian is in the back, a seat so big we referred to it as the rolling couch. My sister Kim is riding shotgun up front with me on our way to visit Mom. Kim suggests taking the Bronx River Parkway.

Unfamiliar with the route, Kim indicates the exit for the entrance to the parkway. The exit is difficult; getting off one highway and on to the next I must exit onto a service road and make my way over to the right hand lane to gain access to the entrance ramp of the parkway. Somewhat confused by the service road, I go slowly. The driver of a red compact car gets impatient and comes so close to my car that I have to go onto the shoulder of the exit ramp to let him by. I am annoyed by his rudeness but more worried about getting off the exit ramp and onto the entrance ramp three lanes over in heavy traffic that I don't give the driver much thought. My sister, however, feels strongly about being nudged off the road and gives him the finger.

Reaching the entrance ramp, I accelerate onto the highway. Soon after entering the parkway, cruising along at sixty-five miles per hour in the middle lane, I hear a loud thump. What the hell is that? I wonder. This is a new car; nothing should be dropping out of it.

I look for signs of any debris or bumps in the road but don't see anything unusual. THUMP, THUMP again, louder. I look over at my sister in the passenger seat where the noise is coming from. I can't believe what I see. The driver of the red car is leaning out his driver side window pounding on my sister's window! His car is so close to mine that I hold my breath. THUMP, THUMP. His face is contorted by so much rage he looks possessed. He must be; he is driving sixty-five mph while pounding on my car window on a busy city parkway!

I am afraid his car is going to slam into mine; it is a miracle that it hasn't already. I glance over to my left. There is a car in the left lane, and I can't go there. I look in the rear view mirror, and there is a car right behind me too. I can't go right; the maniac is there. And in front is another car.

Even if I could accelerate, I don't want this crazy person chasing me. Oddly enough, while I assess the situation, I am calm. I decide to take my foot off the accelerator so I can slow down gradually, and the car behind me doesn't have to hit the brakes hard. While my car slows down, I inch over to the left as far as I can to avoid the madman.

My slowing down and his inability to reach my car seem to infuriate the red car driver even more. I don't know what he wants by pounding on the window. He has our attention, but what does he want? Suddenly the red car swerves right in front of me, missing my right front fender by inches. He is trying to kill us! That is what he wants!

My sister and I watch as the red car swerves into the left lane in front of us. The driver brakes hard to avoid the left lane guardrail and swerves back towards us. His car fishtails — and his back end hits the car that is on our left. That car pushes the red car into the middle lane where it is hit by the car in front of me. The impact of the second hit pushes the red car back toward the left guardrail. BANG! The red car smacks into the left guardrail, tilts up, over, and flips onto its roof and into the middle lane. The red car spins along the pavement while upside down until it is facing the oncoming traffic and stops directly in front of my car.

In sharp contrast to the speed at which the red car bounced off automobiles and crashed, my deceleration appears in slow motion as I come to a full stop two feet from the red car. The driver is upside down and looking straight at my sister and me. His face no longer looks contorted, but his expression seems to say he blames us for the whole disastrous episode — no ownership of his own instant karma.

I look through my windshield and take in the three smashed cars and a three-lane highway at a complete halt. I hear sirens in the distance and watch a few cars pull over to the right hand shoulder to wait for the police. I maneuver my car around the insane man in front of me and drive away. I decided giving the police any personal information in an accident report might end up in the red car driver's hands. The mad man tried to kill us once. Why not again? Besides, there wasn't a scratch on my car — there was no accident to report.

* * *

Joe had an idea that getting together for a spiritual weekend needn't cost anything. We could gather without a teacher. So we invited people from the Wisdom Group to our house later that month for a casual get together. The first day was hectic with people arriving at different times and getting everyone settled. Luckily the weather was beautiful, and people chatted out by the pool, drinking beer, snacking on fruit, chips and homemade salsa.

We made a trip to the ocean where the wind had picked up; only the kids went in the water. The rest of us walked along the water's edge or sat on beach chairs and continued to shoot the breeze. I brought homemade cupcakes, which proved to be a big hit. After enjoying the ocean, Joe barbequed chicken, and we ate together family style around the kitchen table. Everybody slept over; we had people on every couch and spare bed. The next morning Joe and I rise early and make coffee. Eventually everyone wakes up and makes their way to our upstairs deck. Feeling more relaxed now that dinner and all that entails is behind me, I reckon making breakfast for the gang will be much easier. Before we eat, Joe asks, at my request, that we all gather in the living room to meditate.

Nine of us sit on the floor, the couch or on a dining room chair and join hands to say the Circle of Fire prayer. My hands are holding tight onto their hands, a clasp I am unable to ease without great effort. I choose not to fret about my hearty grip, and as I move my attention away from my hands, I notice my heart is beating extremely fast and erratically. The energy I usually feel as heat in a circle has this time gone directly to my heart. The tiny electrical shocks cause my heart to beat like corn popping in a microwave oven.

No one is leading the meditation, so I wait a few moments and squeeze each hand I am holding and let go. I open my eyes and look across the lopsided circle into Joe's big blue eyes. I make the suggestion that we send our teacher our gratitude for having created the connection that has brought us together this morning and ring the Tibetan bells to start our meditation.

My thoughts are far fewer and more spaced apart than usual. I focus on my heart and remember how explosive my heartbeat was when we held hands a few minutes ago. The recent memory invokes a pleasant vision of dots connected by a string of white light. The dots are implied but not visible; instead white lines of light bend at various angles at the point of connection. A few thoughts threaten to drift in and dissolve the image, but the feeling of connection is too appealing for me to give into the usual past-future thought pattern with which I am all too familiar. I imagine the connections we establish in this group growing and linking to more people. This vision gives way to a soft darkness. The darkness reminds me of the soft blackness I encountered before meeting the gremlin of my rejected self.

This soft darkness is similar but not the same. The feeling of connectedness becomes more palpable, and a wave of gratitude comes over me — I am blessed, feel blessed. The soft blackness is filled with my emotions of gratitude and connectedness. My mind gives way to the waves of gratitude, connection and awareness. Fully immersed in the emotion emanating from and through me, my awareness uncouples from my body. I am unbound and limitless. Now, rather than feeling connected to the others in the room, I experience myself as part of them, entering them and expanding beyond them. The soft blackness is the medium, and I am the life force that exists in it. I am formless and aware of a world without form. I know the soft blackness to be nothingness — to be the void I have been afraid of experiencing. But there is no fear in this moment.

I am unlimited and unbounded and joyful and unafraid. I flow through every particle of matter by being nothing but life. I experience being formless while conscious. This is not something I am imagining; I am life without form, life with out boundaries. I understand that all of the teachings that have resonated with me have coalesced into now. My gratitude for the moment floods my awareness as I accept the gift I am given.

Is this the presence of being, the mystery that lies beyond our human condition that Deepak and so many teachers have spoken of? The only answer I get is our dog's Koko's bark. Koko's bark brings me back to my body and to my feet so I can quiet him before he can disturb the others. I don't mind. I could not be more filled with gratitude for the experience, the gift, and with love for the people sitting in my living room.

When the house is empty again I take a nap after writing in my journal about the morning's astonishing adventure. Upon awakening, I am aware of re-inhabiting my body. I do not physically experience the vibrations as I did at Omega last week, but prior to becoming conscious of my surroundings — the couch, the room and who I am — I feel. I feel terror becoming and inhabiting form again.

Hand on heart; I wait for the pounding to stop. I stretch out on the couch after coming into full consciousness. I'm more curious than disturbed — never before have I noticed an emotion when becoming aware of my body while waking up. Usually there is a physical sensation, a blankness of memory, then a grasping for identity. This afternoon I am aware of terror first, then the thought of form, the sensation of re-entering form, and then the realization of identity. I roll over and decide not to get up. I fall back asleep, wondering what I will experience waking up next time. I wake up to the same experience; awareness of terror, awareness of form, and finally an understanding of identity.

I write about the terror in my journal. While writing, I begin to laugh as I remember a scene in the Walt Disney movie *Aladdin*. I hear Robin Williams' voice as the Genie while he is being sucked back into his bottle, "Big powerful genie — tiny little bottle."

Named unnamed

A YOUNG MAN IN OMEGA'S BOOKSTORE RECOMMENDED TENZIN WANGYAL Rinpoche's, a Tibetan lama of the Bon tradition, dream yoga book last year. The idea of practicing meditation while sleeping was too attractive to pass up. As a working mother, I reasoned sleeping was a great time to meditate; if I could get away with it. The book was actually about how the dream and sleep state are similar to the transition from one life to the next. According to the book, if a person can stay aware while they are dreaming and sleeping, when they die they have a better chance of staying aware in that state too. When they die they are more aware and are able to choose a more desirable situation for the next life.

I must admit I do wonder how much luck goes into where and to whom a person is born. Fairness, by human standards, is certainly not a factor. Did I have any influence in coming into this life? Is my comfortable life, by any standard, an accident? Born in the wealthiest nation in the world during a sustained period of peace has its advantages. Why me, here and now?

The Sprain Brook Parkway is a beautiful stretch of road. The bucolic landscape, reflected in the small river, speeds along beside me. Trees and sky are paralleled flawlessly in the dark green glassy water. Tenzin Wangyal Rinpoche said there are thousands of things in a day that can send the message: "This is a dream." Rinpoche told us to get used to saying, "This is a dream," while awake. Our dreams should contain messages that let us know we are dreaming. Instead of looking for

143

hands, a Toltec tool in lucid dreaming, or blinking lights, a scientific method for lucid dreaming, there are lots of things when encountered in a dream that give you the message: "This is a dream." Encapsulated in my air-conditioned van, speeding along on serpentine pavement, mesmerized by the movement of sky, trees and clouds above and beside me, all in mirrored perfection, I tell myself, "This is a dream."

This life is a dream. I create my dream life, and I leave messages in my dream to 'wake up.' Wake up to the reality of my being? Maybe. Life as we experience it awake is a dream, an illusion. What is real is something else.

Joe sends an e-mail from work later in the week with a link to *The Divinity of the Human Soul* by Swami Omkarananda. Surprised and delighted that he is searching the web for spiritual wisdom, I don't know what to reply back. Is this really my husband Joe, sending me this e-mail? I particularly like one part of the article and print it out to take home:

'Dharma' means nature, motive, law. What is the Dharma of the earth? To attract the apples on the tree by the law of gravitation. The law of gravitation is its Dharma, its nature. Whatever you throw up is pulled down to earth. What is the Dharma of a person? To go back to the experience of the Absolute. There is but one goal, one law, the law of evolution, the law of self-realization, god-experience.

Whatever is born has to experience the Divine. This is the single central motive. This motive takes divergent forms. The search for unending happiness, the search for indestructible peace, the search for more and more wealth, all are nothing but an expression of the search for God. For all these are characteristics of the Divine and one cannot have peace, happiness, beauty, and so on without God-experience. Our only Dharma is to attract the Infinite. The Infinite attracts us in millions of ways.

August 2003

The services in the summer are informal, so I have boldly not written anything down for the sermon. We are to speak about our favorite Unitarian Universalist principle. I chose number four — A Free and Responsible Search for Truth. I am drawn to the principle; for me the principle emphasizes that I am responsible for my spiritual journey. Not the minister of this fellowship, not the Unitarian Universalist Association, not even God. I am responsible to search out my spiritual truth. I am responsible to look far and near for meaning in my life. A free and responsible search for truth is a unique religious principle in our world, and I cherish its place among the seven principles of Unitarian Universalism.

I bring Cari Cole's CD and play *Beautiful Life* for those who have come to listen, share and worship together. There is no need for a pulpit today; we sit in a circle facing one another. I read the first line of *Cherish Your Doubts* by Robert T. Weston and wait for the responding voices. *Cherish your doubts, for doubt is the attendant of truth.*[3]

I picked this reading from the hymnal because that is how my journey began for me — with doubts. Doubts about what I believed, what I thought was important, what was real, what I was feeling.

I follow up with another reading and response called *It Matters What We Believe* by Sophia Lyon Fahs. It does matter what I believe. What I believe creates the lens I see the world through. Doubts are okay, because I can change what I believe; the history of the human race is one long story of belief, doubt, change, new belief, doubt and change. The reading and response is a lesson in itself and I enjoy hearing the light and dark of the opposing stanzas.

> *Some beliefs are like blinders, shutting off the power to choose one's own direction.*
> *Other beliefs are like gateways opening wide vistas for exploration.*[4]

Poems, stories and music from around the globe are shared; Rumi, a Sufi Mystic, *Becoming the Lotus* from the Egyptian Book of the Dead, Walt Whitman, Buddha, and John from the New Testament. I conclude the service with a quote from the Chandogya Upanishad, which highlights so succinctly what can happen when we fail to search for truth within our own heart and mind.

> *You could have golden treasure buried beneath your feet, and walk over it again and again, yet never find it because you don't realize it is there. Just so, all beings live every moment in the city of the Divine, but never find the Divine because it is hidden by the veil of illusion.*

My summer ends with Jed McKenna's book *Spiritual Enlightenment — The Damnedest Thing.* His view of enlightenment reminds me of what I experienced at fourteen — the hole, the emptiness, the nothing inside of existence. That afternoon so long ago I remember how impossible it was having a discussion about God with Mom. She was so sure about God. Not me, we could have made him up, and if we made him up out of a need for a great protector, then what else did we make up?

Looking through the open bathroom door, exasperated with her dogmatic responses, I caught a glimpse of myself in the bathroom mirror and wondered who made me. I spied a glimpse of another image of myself in the mirror. The mirror on the wall behind me was reflecting back the image of me sitting on the stairs looking into the bathroom mirror. The mirrors are aligned just enough to create an infinity reflection of myself, reflecting on myself.

For a moment my mind grasped the idea that I could be creating myself, my life, God, reality — existence itself. I blinked and stood up, nauseous, as if suffering from motion sickness. Behind the queasiness was a profound loneliness coupled with a feeling of isolation in a sea of nothingness. I would not go there — no way, too frightening — and slammed the door to that possibility, closed.

But as the memory comes back to me today the fear I experienced at fourteen is gone. I wasn't prepared last time I took a glance at the possibilities of my own creative existence. I glean McKenna is telling the reader that to abide in non-dual awareness is to abide in the abyss. Except there is no 'you;' the center of the onion is nothing. The true self is no self.

Meditating regularly reveals I am everything and nothing. I sense it with a myopic I-fixation that is coupled with the hollow nothingness at my core. If I am self-reflective and brutally honest, these are the two states at either end of my human awareness of self. But I'm curious. Is it a unique human paradox that both states of being are equally true?

Lying in my pool on a spectacular end-of-summer day thinking about existence, I wonder if all this exists? I take in the water, the trees, the sun, the wood deck, the blue, blue sky above me and receive an answer:

'*I*' *do not exist.*

I smile a non-existent smile and feel comfortable with the idea and float aimlessly while the sun seeps into my bones and cool water laps at my feet. I receive an answer to a question not asked:

'*I*' *am intent, some thing or no-thing's intent.*

This is
the truth
that passes
understanding

Lunchtime in New York City looking for a watch battery, I make my way down to the jewelry district off Sixth Avenue about seven blocks from my office. The streets are crowded thanks to the drop in humidity that the end of summer brings. My head is occupied with dream theories; if life is nothing but a dream, then this is an awfully long dream. Hmmmm, yes, unless we go on for eternity and each lifetime is a dream.

Whoa!

Measured by eternity, lifetimes would be short dreams — a series of dreams through out an endless night. But are they disconnected? I wonder. Maybe that is what recapitulation is for, finding the threads in this lifetime that connect past and future lifetimes. What about waking up? Ending Karma? What is there when there is no dream? Enlightenment? Turning the corner I glance up and spy **99 DREAMS 99.**

Across the street is a new five and dime shop with the word, DREAMS, in two-foot red neon letters above its front door. How bizarre is that! 99 Dreams splashed in front of my face while having this conversation in my head. Coincidence? Deepak Chopra says coincidence is God's mind at work. God is a funny man today. And perhaps I have left myself a message to remind me that this life is but a dream.

148

September 2003

Usually I get to the game an hour early like most parents. The coaches insist the players arrive an hour before start time. The players warm-up, weigh in and go over plays. Today Joe took Garrett to the field by himself. Going in separate cars lets Joe leave early for the Jets game, and I don't have to hang out at the field for an hour before the game. Not that there will be too many more mornings spent doing that. This is Garrett's last season playing football for PAL.

Garrett begged us to let him play six years ago; his new friend in our new neighborhood was on the team. I remember the first time I signed the boys up; the helmets and pads where almost as big as they were. It took twenty minutes to suit them up before every practice and game. As cute and small as they were that first season, they learned to play ball. Even at seven and eight the coaches took football seriously, some a little too seriously. The parents, of course, are even worse. I'm worse than a coach when it is game time. Monday morning quarterbacking is nothing compared to what a mom on the sidelines does during a game in which one of her kids is playing.

I walk past a bathroom on the way to the field, a luxury most of the ballparks don't have. How the boys can last sometimes three or four hours without peeing amazes me. They are squeezed into tight spandex with kidney pads and athletic cups and are doing sit-ups and leg lifts and drinking Gatorade and running and hitting — but no peeing. I have to give up my second cup of coffee for these games. No bathroom facility means limiting liquid intake in the morning.

I find Joe on the sidelines and stand next to him. We don't sit much at these games. We move up and down the field to follow the ball like the players do. Sometimes I will stand up on the top step of the bleachers so I can see the whole field, but by the end of the game, I am on the ground as close to the field as the referees let the parents get. Sometimes there is a fence separating us from the field and the players. Not a bad idea really. Some of us are vicious and what comes out of our mouths is better not heard by the kids.

We won the toss and will have first possession for the first game of the last season. Last year was tough. We had been division champs two years prior so the league put our town in the A division. We were playing against organizations that had sixty, seventy kids to choose from and made cuts. Those teams would walk on the field, and I would sink into myself a little. Each player looked athletic, confident and fit. Our team accepted everybody; if you showed up, you played. We had all sizes — tall, short, pudgy, skinny and scrappy. While the competition was warming up in NFL fashion, some of our kids were eating bagels on the bench.

We lost most games last season. One game we didn't even get a first down. But each kid showed up at every game unless he was sick or had broken something. They played the game to the end, even when there wasn't a chance in hell they could score, let alone win. Andrew and Garrett never once mentioned quitting, even though they both had doubts about playing that year at the beginning of the season. They stuck it out and had a thousand times more grace about the season than any of the parents or coaches.

Andrew isn't playing on the team this year; he is too old. There is a twelve-year-old cut off. Garrett is playing Andrew's old position, fore-back. A tough position, mostly blocking so another running back can get through the opponents linemen.

Andrew paid his dues for three years in that position and almost never got the ball. Block, block, block. One of the few circumstances where blocking is seen as a positive action. I wasn't happy when Garrett told me the coach gave him Andrew's old position. Garrett deserved better, I thought, he deserves to get the ball more. I don't want to go through another season steaming on the sidelines because my kid never gets the ball.

Oh, well, there is nothing I can do, let go, let go, detach, I tell myself. Yeah, well, whoever advised letting go never had their kid on sports teams; I argue with no one, in defense of my attachment to the game. Breathe in, breathe out, watch the game and stay away from the other moms, I advise myself during the opening play. Together we can sink into a negative tirade against the stupid coaches: how they don't know how to call the right plays, and how they don't give the right kids the ball at the right time, and how they never try anything new, and how their sons always get the good plays and, and, and . . .

. . . And it is first quarter. We have the ball, and we are moving down field, second down and seventeen yards from the end zone. The quarterback, a coach's son, receives the snap, drops back and hands off the ball to Garrett as Garrett laterals around in the backfield. Garrett continues going to the outside, sees a hole, breaks through the line and heads for the end zone. Head up, ball tucked, long thoroughbred legs pumping hard, he outruns the opponents' defense and sails over the goal line. We are screaming and jumping and screaming. My heart is bursting. The first touchdown of the first game of the last season, and my baby scores! Life doesn't get any better than moments like this.

October 2003

I signed up for this particular workshop because of the description on the flyer I received in the mail. *The meditative practices of Dzogchen are designed to stabilize the mind to enable us to discover our innate awareness and to experience boundlessness, spontaneity and flexibility in thought, meditation and life.* I've experienced boundlessness once and want to know how to do it again. Tenzin Wangyal Rinpoche is teaching, so I hope he can help me. His dream yoga exercises work for the most part, and I am anxious to hear how to practice boundlessness.

He talks of space and the properties of space. How space equals open awareness. No preconceptions. Space allows everything. He explains how you must create space for something new to happen. He asks us to picture a clear blue sky over a wide-open desert landscape before leading us in a round of chanting meditations. He asks us to meditate on an obstacle in our life. An obstacle is like a cloud in our blue sky he says. The blue sky is space, the potential for all, and the cloud is our perceived obstacle preventing us from reaching our potential. TW Rinpoche tells us to clear our obstacle out of the space by connecting to the antidote of the problem. After connecting with the antidote, radiate out the antidote from your heart.

The obstacle I would most like to remove is my worrying about money and a job. Being a consultant, having quit my full time job, I don't have the same security as an employee. I have been training my client's employees to do my job. Something I didn't used to do, as it obviously makes my presence there less necessary. I want to pass on what I know, so that another working mom can do what I did, parlay the knowledge into a lucrative part-time work arrangement. Besides, I don't want to do tax work forever. But I make really good money. What am I going to do without the kind of money I currently make? I spend a lot of useless time worrying about money. I don't want to waste any more energy worrying about jobs and money.

To help clear the space, we chant the sound Ah, the Tibetan letter A. We are to visualize clearing the space by projecting out from our forehead. To help us connect with an antidote, we chant the sound Om while concentrating on the throat area. And finally we radiate out that antidote from our heart while chanting the Hung sound. Hearing thirty-five people releasing the same sound over and over helps me stay present in the meditation. The vibrations in my throat and mouth resonate internally as I exhale the ahhh sound along with the people around me. Our unique vibrations meld together near the end of the ahhh, and I listen to the different intensities as each person inhales before the next round begins. Our teacher is always the first to start the round and usually the last to inhale before beginning again.

As I chant Ahh, I meditate on what might be the antidote to my worries about work and money. The antidote is trust. I need to trust life. I need to trust myself. When it is time to radiate out I stay present, do my best and let my worries go as soon as they come up.

During the second round, I am able to hover on the vibrating sound coming from my throat and relax into the group energy so that my mind stays open and uncluttered by the usual junk. I feel a force press down on my right breast, a presence I perceive as a spirit wanting to come in. While exhaling a full and satisfying ahhhh, I invite the spirit in, letting the unfamiliar presence know there are no secrets here. I follow the spirit when it leaves my body, and I enter the woman on my left on her next inhaled breath. Inside of her, I mix with her blood and am released with her exhale of ahhhh.

Near the end of the third round of meditations, I turn my attention towards the teacher. I feel his energy as he continues to lead us through the last round of chants. I feel that He is Me. I am conscious of a melding of identity as I release the air from my lungs through my throat and out my mouth. I am carried, and then dissolve, in my own breath. I hear our blended Oms and know that I am they, and they are me.

During a break, I can't resist asking the teacher a question, the question I have wanted to ask since I first arrived but don't feel comfortable asking in front of the other students. I wait for the person kneeling next to TW Rinpoche to finish, and I approach.

Rinpoche is sitting on cushions, and I don't think he gets up once during the breaks. I make a slight bow and put my hands together in prayer position. I have no idea if there is a protocol for approaching Rinpoche with a question. I am not even sure how to address him. I ask a question I don't really care about to warm up. Then I lower my head and ask, as I glance at him through my eyelashes, "Can you become the space?"

"Yes," he says immediately.

I exhale with relief and tell him that it happened to me this summer, and I don't know why or how it happened, but I became space while meditating. I tell him that is why I came to his workshop this weekend.

He nods knowingly and tells me transcendent occurrences happen spontaneously when we practice.

There are other devotees waiting, and I don't know what else to say that could add anything to his definitive answer. I make another little bow while backing away and thanking him. It *was* real, I say to myself. A Tibetan master has validated my boundlessness.

TW Rinpoche tells us that the problem we perceive as an obstacle is really a manifestation of a deeper problem which is really the only problem — and that is ignorance. It is the ignorance that causes the obscuration of self. I see my obstacles as veils of illusion that keep me from trusting myself. Not the little me with a job, house and minivan, but the boundless me, the dissolve into space me; the space — spirit — TW Rinpoche who is me, me.

While the teacher summarizes the weekend and mentions the blue sky visualization again, I envision myself by my pool with a cloudless blue sky above me. I see the green leaves on the trees around the pool contrasting brilliantly against the blue, blue sky. The view doesn't look quite real. It is perfection. I can look out and see the sky, trees and water as if they are framed in a postcard from a friend's vacation. I look down and spot my bare foot at the end of my lounge chair, and now it too is part of the postcard. Now a part of me is in the picture, but I know the foot isn't me. I am what is aware of the postcard. My body can be in the postcard, but I cannot; I am the awareness of my body, the trees, the water and the sky. If I reach out my hand to touch my foot, my hand also becomes part of the postcard. But I cannot reach myself — I am no thing, no form. I am awareness. Even the thought of the postcard is not me. I am the awareness of the thought of the metaphor of the postcard.

The morning after the workshop, Joe and the boys eat breakfast before going off to school. I pour myself a second cup of coffee and join them at the table. Andrew is eating a strawberry Pop-Tart. The smell is so tantalizing that I can't believe the Pop-Tart tastes as bad as it does.

Garrett has his day planner open and is stuffing his homework into the folder pockets in between spoonfuls of cinnamon toast crunch cereal. Joe starts putting the dishes in the dishwasher while urging the boys to go upstairs and brush their teeth. I turn my head to look out the window and see an abandoned industrial site with weeds and boarded up brick windows. It takes me a moment to realize I am on the train on my way to work. Wow, I visited home while dreaming between Jamaica and Hunterspoint Avenue.

Home was so real; I can't help feeling that I was really there. I don't remember falling asleep, but I do remember thinking of Joe and the boys and their morning routine. I guess I popped in for a visit. I am reminded of the Tibetan Dream Yoga books I have read. Both books assert that once you are lucid in your dream and control the events you can go anywhere. In my dreams I create everything. In this wakefulness state I am only aware of my reactions to my perceptions, which are in effect another creation. Both states are empty and are filled by me. Is the goal of enlightenment to perceive without the baggage of interpretation and judgment? Are we ultimately here to help create the world and enjoy with human awareness the gift of life?

Why compassion and love then? Are love and compassion a judgment call? Or are they another way of perceiving? Buddhists say compassion leads to the end of samsara, the cyclical illusion of birth, death and suffering. Does that mean no compassion extends and perpetuates samsara, the illusion of suffering and death? I don't know. I have to catch a very real Number 7 train into Manhattan and am reacting badly to the perception of having to buy another Metrocard this morning, since I can't find the one I purchased last week.

I usually work on Thursdays, but I take the next day off to watch Andrew play football. He joined the Middle School team this year, and

I want to see as many games as I can. He has practice every day except Sunday. Even though he is third string and there are sixty boys on the team, he shows up to every practice. I can see the difference in his attitude towards school, since he has joined the team. He hasn't missed a day — and he appears confident and relaxed with his friends this year. I hope he gets to play today. Sometimes he doesn't even get on the field. The team is undefeated, but the coaches leave the first and second string players in, if there is even a whiff of competition in the air.

I find a spot on the bleachers, high enough to see the whole field but low enough so the rest of the bleachers block the wind behind me. Damn, I forgot a bleacher blanket, but I remembered my gloves. I should be okay. The sun is out thankfully but will be gone by the time the game is over. It gets pretty chilly when the last bit of warm light fades down below the top of the bleachers. I settle in for the first half. He almost never gets in the first half; I enjoy the game without any personal stake, other than Andrew's team is playing; and I hope they win. But I don't really care; that is not what I come for.

Fourth quarter, and my son enters the game — and then the other team has the ball. The quarterback fakes a throw and slips the ball to a running back. There is a flurry of jerseys as the linemen clash and block each other into a stalemate. Wait, wait, the running back got through on the far side, the kid with the ball made it through, 5 yards, 10 yards, he is out in front, and nobody is between him and the end zone. This is the closest the other team has come to scoring, and this time they might make it.

"Get him, get him!" I shriek. I see a yellow jersey, number 14, from our team break out and run after the player with the ball. Number 14 is gaining, stretching, every part of him intent on bringing down the ball carrier. The gap closes but the end zone is almost within reach. Number 14 leaps into the air, arms outstretched, and grabs his opponent's hips and jersey — and holds on while they crash to the ground together. The stands erupt in a roar of approval. I jump into the air and yell, "Yeah, baby, that's it!"

Andrew, number 14, took down his opponent like a lion on the open prairie brings down its prey. I breathe in the crisp fall air, juiced up and satisfied. This is why I come to the games. I love the rawness. I love the raw physicalness of the game — the basic animal instinct and raw emotional aspect of the tackle. I love when a kid gets the ball, makes it past the linemen and runs down the field and scores, but I like it even better when one of my own takes them down.

With joy
we claim
the growing light

THIS GROUP HAS BROUGHT ME TO MEDITATION LEVELS I DON'T THINK I COULD have reached on my own, but we only spend a few minutes a day on meditation. I am having trouble following whatever the teacher is attempting to impart to us this Mystica retreat weekend, but I enjoy the other women — and dressing up for Halloween is fun.

I recreate an image of myself in a dream I had a few years ago. In the dream I was screaming at my brother Eric and caught a glimpse of myself in a mirror. My anger had caused my temple veins to be vibrantly visible under my skin, blue lighting bolts running from my scalp to the corners of my eyes. Fascinated by my reflection, I forgot my anger and brother completely. Dramatic and other worldly, I thought I wouldn't mind looking that way in waking life. Well, tonight is my chance. I trace lightening bolts in electric blue eyeliner from my scalp to the corners of my eyes. After spiking my hair with gooey gel, I throw a handmade veil around my shoulders. Coincidentally the glued-on glitter symbols in the veil are the same color as my bright blue veins. The look is original, if not exactly frightening.

We wait on the starlit deck for our turn to sit in front of the teacher. She is dressed in black and wears a screen mask that hides the features of her face. Last, I wait on the deck alone and feel the following solidify in my mind. *I am a warrior. I serve no being but God. Freedom from tyranny, all tyranny is my cause and purpose.* Moments later sitting across the coffee table from my teacher, I accept the notion that we have been friends for thousands of years. She takes off her mask, and we smile at each other; no words are spoken, no words are needed.

We end the weekend in a circle in a sunlit living room. Outside the expansive windows is a panoramic view of a calm lake surrounded by lush foliage. No expense was spared this time on our Tennessee accommodations. I will miss these women. A connection is being severed; I do not believe I will have the time or money to spend on Mystica retreats anymore. I have decided to participate in Toltec Dreaming every month for a year instead.

I have spent so little time with them but feel an attachment that is deep and satisfying. During the final group meditation, I relax and sit with no expectations. I reach out to each woman with my heart to say goodbye. When I reach the wizard I am met with a swirling and decidedly erotic burst of energy. We entwine our energies, and our ethereal dancing hug is so tangible that I pull back slightly out of surprise and delight. I reach out to the meditation teacher and my energy is enveloped in a warm loving embrace. There is no mistaking the intermingling of our personal energy bodies. Oh, I will miss that! How did we do it? I do not get a chance to ask; the meditation is over. Everyone is hugging in the physical now and the moment has passed.

Later in the week I meditate about time, each moment a bubble. I see an ocean of bubbles, dark luminescent, purplish-blue iridescent bubbles. I envision myself moving through the bubbles, moving through time. Living moment-to-moment, letting moments arise, acknowledging them and then letting the bubble-moment float by. I am flowing through time; time is not passing by me. When I grasp onto a moment — a bubble, it makes for a jerky journey. When I hold on I get weighed down. I don't know where I am going. I am concerned with collecting the bubbles I have passed.

The potential for every future always exists but is not determined until I choose to move this way or that through the bubbles of time. Interdependence and co-existence creates an infinite number of combinations of moments and experiences that are constantly being rearranged with every choice. How I perceive the passage of time is characteristic of how I move through the day: jerking or smooth — slow and painful or effortlessly flowing; grasping or detaching — collecting and resisting or accepting and letting go.

November 2003

I received an e-mail about *The Harmonic Concordance*. The upcoming full moon eclipse will be accompanied by the alignment of several planets and a star configured in the shape of two inverted pyramids. The e-mail asks people to celebrate the event by Om-ing at a specific time. Their hope is to use this rare astrological occurrence to raise consciousness and form connections throughout as many groups of people as possible.

I forwarded the e-mail to Grace, my Yoga teacher, and she said she would open her home, if I would lead the group. Not the response I expected, but I thanked her for opening her home and told her I would lead the ceremony, though I had no idea what to do other than the Om-ing instructions in the e-mail. Actually I am glad to have been asked. I get to create a ritual. How cool is that?

The day of the eclipse I click into one of the web sites linked in the e-mail and select an excerpt to share called *Linking with the Divine.*

> . . . It is time to step free of fears and the myriad of belief patterns that keep us so boxed in our world of structure and control. Time to move forward in trust and faith knowing there are worlds beyond that which we can see with our ears.[5]

Later that night we gather in a circle in Grace's yoga studio. A Rumi poem sets the mood. I have found when in doubt what to offer up spiritually, recite Rumi.

> Keep knocking and the joy inside will eventually
> Open a window and look out to see who is there.

I sound first at exactly the time specified. We open our mouths and let out an OOOHHHHMMM. Each of us gathered has different lung capacities — we end and begin at different times. Round and round we go. At first the sound is contentious, and nothing at all like the blending of Oms I am used to at the end of Grace's yoga class. I worry that we will not be able to continue for twenty minutes; we are almost breathless at times. I let those thoughts go and resolve to see the ritual through. I concentrate on my own chanting and find a rhythm and breathing cycle that relaxes me. I notice as I relax the surrounding chants compliment my voice, though the Oms are not timed or in tune with me. What began as a jumble of discordant voices becomes a small melody of desire and life. Each person creates their own timbre and rhythm while winding in and out of a circle of never ending Oms.

We chant Om with thousands of others around the world, then walk out to Grace's deck and watch the clear red moon eclipse to nothingness and reform in reflected light once again. I pray for the harmony we Om-ed into existence to permeate the earth. I believe we are on the cusp of a new age. An age so new that most don't recognize it. It is only in looking back, that I realize how different things really are.

December 2003

I wake up in a cabin bunk bed trying to remember the wispy fragments of a dream before they dissolve into solid thoughts. The more I try to remember, the more awake I become, and any chance of reconstructing the dream or its message evaporates like vapor in sunlight. The room is still dark but now quiet, the anonymous snorer has given me a reprieve. This is the first time we have shared a room with other couples, usually Joe and I have a room to ourselves during the Wisdom Group retreats. I don't mind — except for the snoring. Whoever it is, is loud; and I want to fall back asleep before he starts up again.

Unable to sleep, I review the changes in my life. I see my life as a movie, and I have the starring role. At one level of awareness I am able to watch myself as I participate in the movie. As the spiral of my spiritual path unfolded, I became aware that I am creating the movie as well as watching and participating. But the me that is creating this life-movie is unknown to me. I do not know that part of myself, the creator-self.

I extrapolate further and realize that the goal is for me to eventually know the part of me that not only created the dream I live but every dream that is every human life, the creator of all, everything. *Phoot, phoot, phoot, phoot,* lives replicating like a deck of cards dealt out by a magician and expanding out into space is the image that appears in my mind's eye. I feel each *phoot* sound resonate in my cells. Each dream a human life replicated from a single source. All one but divided into endless unique creations.

I make my way through the sleeping bodies to the bathroom and turn on the light I need to write in my journal. The epiphany accompanied by visions and surround sound seems so clear in the middle of the night — sensible, comprehensive and profound. The next morning when the teacher starts explaining to the newcomers the work we do at the retreats I raise my hand and ask to share what I wrote in the bathroom a few hours ago. I never know exactly how what I communicate is received. Crystal clear to me, I wonder if anybody else knows what I am talking about or can understand what is coming through me and being given to them.

Later in the day we dream of forgiveness. We are asked to visualize ourselves at an empty beach. We are told to look down the vacant beach and the person we need the most to forgive will walk towards us. I see my mother coming to me over the sand. We meet, and I hug her frail body next to mine. I am careful of her delicate hollow back, a side effect of the emphysema that leaves her wheezing for breath. We hug with an emotion I don't feel capable of most of the time when I am with her in the flesh. I am grateful for these moments of kindness between us. I am grateful that we are not exchanging the petty offenses with which we indulge ourselves.

I kiss her cheek and release her. The sun and sand fill my imagination again, and I remember that Mom doesn't care much for the beach. I imagine a colorful beach umbrella and lounge chair and help my mother into the shade. I imagine an ice cold martini and pass the elegant olive spiked glass to her, knowing she will enjoy the visit more with a cocktail in her hand.

I sit in the sand beside the lounge chair and hold her free hand. I want to stay like this for a while, close and peaceful. I have forgiven my mother, but now I must forgive myself. I must forgive that little girl who wanted more. I wanted more back then and felt terrible for wanting more. I wanted a calmer, consistently attentive Mom. I wanted a lap to sit on, not someone who worried about their dress getting wrinkled. I wanted more but felt the ungrateful brat when I admitted I wanted more to myself.

I need to forgive myself for wanting more. To accept that it is okay to want more love, more comfort, more safety as a child. Joe comes to mind, and I realize that when I was able, I did give myself more. I dreamed

Joe into my life — big, warm, loyal, loveable Joe, my husband and spiritual companion. It has taken me almost twenty years to appreciate the gift that I have given myself with Joe. I understand now that I fulfilled my desire for more by saying yes to Joe and all his love for me.

I am suspended in awe for the creator of my life. The me who is wise enough to find my heart's desire before I am aware of what that desire even is. I want to know more about the life creator that is me. I want to know myself. I want more.

Since what we choose is what we are

I THINK OF MY FATHER WHEN I FIND MYSELF LIKING MY WINE TOO MUCH. SUCH A pleasant habit — that hazy buzz of alcohol easing a frazzled mind into neutral after a long day at work. Not drunk, mind you, that is altogether different. My father asked me what I thought of him in probably the last genuine discussion I had with him before he died suddenly from his third heart attack. It was an unexpected question. He never appeared to care what his family thought of him before. The ensuing conversation was totally out of character for him. We didn't have conversations, my father and I.

I loved my father out of loyalty and compassion, not out of respect or admiration. I told him the truth, my truth. And while it seems harsh in retrospect, I was pulling my punches that night. I soft pedaled my anger and told him I thought he didn't live his life to his full potential. That he could have done more, given his intelligence and hard work. From his perspective, life looked like it took him for a ride, abandoned by his biological father at birth and raised by an overworked mother and a cold unloving stepfather. His first wife, my mother, was profoundly unhappy while married. He had six children to feed, one child a schizophrenic and another struggled with a learning disability. But the choice was still his every time his hand lifted a drink to his mouth.

That's what I remember the most; the drink in his hand, his eye on the bar TV screen and the numb waste that he became when he drank. Some people say addicts don't have a choice. I think that is bullshit. Some addicts quit and others, at some level, choose not to quit.

I dream infrequently of my father since his death. When I do dream of him there is always an associated sense of guilt. Why am I feeling guilty? Wasn't he the one who broke promises again and again? Wasn't he the cause of our family embarrassment and financial woes? Isn't he the one who drove my mother to the edge of madness with his selfish addiction to alcohol? And if all of this is true, then why does he appear so alone and vulnerable in my dreams?

January 2004

Going through scraps of paper from a box that sits on the credenza in my home office, I find a note I wrote about the message Joe received in France in 2002. Over the years I have stuffed the latched wicker box with ideas that came to me suddenly and seemed, at the time, quite profound. I would write the inspiration on whatever was handy, an old envelope or scrap of paper, and put it into the box. After that I was free to continue the laundry, cook dinner or finish whatever chore I was involved in when the insight hit. I'd never gone back to the box until today.

The note is my interpretation concerning possible creations between males and females. I take a less literal view and believe that when there is a connection between two people something is created. One alone does not create; there needs to be a sending and a receiving. Creation is in the interaction. The millions and billions of connections between ourselves create the world in which we live. The more love sent and received in these connections, the more heaven on earth.

Coincidentally, while meditating earlier this New Year's Day, the word relationship descended into my consciousness. My mind gave way as I basked in the light of the knowledge that existence is in the relationship. The relationship I have with Joe, the boys, my mother, my siblings, my friends, clients, fellow humans, the earth and myself. All of heaven is creatable with my choices, my awareness and my love.

Dreaming with Joe in the following days, I try to empty myself, but can't rid myself of an idea I have about free trade. When the public became aware of dolphins being killed in the tuna nets on the big commercial fishing boats, dolphin safe labels were created and placed on all the tuna cans that were sold by companies that used new nets less abusive to dolphins.

I envision worldwide *Living Wages* and *No Child Labor Used* labels on all of the products made by companies who can make that claim. I want to know, so I can choose, which product to buy based on whether the person making the product, even if they are in China, Indonesia, Mexico or the US, is being paid a living wage.

I know from history books what working conditions were like in this country when there was no threat of empowering workers. Capitalists are not known for their compassion. Let the consumer decide. Labels based on independent auditors findings about worker wages and conditions would go a long way in letting a true free market evolve.

Right now, free trade agreements put all the pressure on competition and none on human and workers' rights. To expect corporations and repressive governments to create more humane working conditions by themselves may be expecting too much. Let demand by choice drive the equation.

I hope that most consumers would choose the product whose label ensured there was no child labor involved. I hope they would choose the product that gives the people who produced the goods a chance for a decent life over a product that cannot make the same claim. Maybe people won't choose that way, but at least they would understand what kind of world they are creating with their choices and their money.

February 2004

Egad! I am quoting the bible and Dr. Seuss in the same service. Is someone rolling over in their grave as I speak? I hope so. I experience a turn on the wheel of life when Garrett reads *What Was I Afraid Of?* to the younger children during Story for all Ages. My mother would read the story about the spooky green pants with nobody inside them to my brother and me. What a treat to have Mom use her silliest voices to bring the characters alive for us when we were little. And what a great story to illustrate my point. What are we really afraid of? I end the service with *Litany of Atonement* by Robert Eller Isaacs. The piece presents a different meaning for atonement, one I had not considered.

Perfect for the sermon, perfect for my ruminations. Perfectly waiting for me to read and understand in the right moment.

For remaining silent when a single voice would have made a difference

We forgive ourselves and each other: we begin again in love.

For each time that our fears have made us rigid and inaccessible

We forgive ourselves and each other: we begin again in love.[6]

The list goes on but always ends with we forgive ourselves and each other and begin again in love. How else to proceed as a human with a human heart?

I open the boys' report cards that arrive by mail. Andrew received another ninety-nine in gym. "How do you get a ninety-nine in gym?" I ask. A quarter inch rise out of one side of his teenage mouth and a slight shrug of his shoulders lets me know he is pleased with the question but not enough to actually answer it. I can't imagine being athletic enough in every sport to get one point away from perfect. I look down at his man-sized feet and wonder if that is the secret to his physical prowess. I use to call him the goat; so surefooted he was as a toddler. He stood up and walked at nine months. I was a little disappointed after awhile, the sweetly funny boom of a toddler's diaper padded butt hitting the ground didn't happen. Andrew robbed me of that; he never fell down.

He still doesn't. We went skiing a few weekends ago and went down some of the green trails together. I was confident by the end of the first day on the intermediate slopes but shied away from the black diamonds. The second morning I followed Andrew to Devil's Bowl instead of staying on the gentler, familiar path. A slight twist of the hip, and he glided down the trail; it might have been a summer stroll instead of a slick, vertical, morning-crusted ski slope.

I skied down after him, frightened of the drop. I slowed down and fell over the moment I told myself I shouldn't be doing this — it's too icy and steep. Gracelessly I propped myself back on my skis, knowing from experience that the only way out was down the hill. So I went, upright and fast. Andrew watched the whole sorry episode. On the lift up he asked me, "Why did you fall when you were hardly even moving?"

"I psyched myself out. I told myself I couldn't do it. So, of course, I couldn't. Then I realized I had to go down the trail anyway, and I did and was fine."

"Yeah," he replied, "you looked good the rest of the way down."

Thinking back, I hope he retained the larger lesson. He can ski gracefully and get a ninety-nine in gym, but high school is around the corner. As a teenager, I worry he may tell himself there are plenty of things he can't do.

March 2004

I had promised to present what I found in *Science and the Search for God,* a book written by Gary Kowalski, a UU minister, after sharing an excerpt in the UUA magazine at a previous service. Kowalski's examination of Quantum Physics in relationship with our evolving conception of God is mind-blowing. Many of his ideas are similarly presented in the movie *What the Bleep Do We Know.* The Vermont minister's take is comprehensively scientific as it is spiritually enlightening.

We examine the question of existence when I quote Stephen Hawking, best-selling author of *A Brief History of Time: From the Big Bang to Black Holes.* Hawking states that even if he and his fellow physicists succeeded in drafting a Grand Unified Theory that encompasses all the laws of nature, they would still not know why the universe goes to the bother of existing. I do not share my vision in Tennessee from almost a year ago or the understanding that we, as a part of the universe, are here to know there is God. I believe it is a truth that should be experienced, not told, even though Kowalski and several quantum physicists have come to the same conclusion. My respect for the Unitarian Universalist faith is deepened as I spread the knowledge from one of its leaders to my fellow worshipers.

May 2004

A thought crystallizes and comes into focus while driving on the Southern State Parkway. *I can only control how I reflect back the gift of life.* My projections, interpretations and actions are the way I reflect life back to the source of life. Everything else is an illusion of control. I visualize life flowing like water through my fingers. Even with cupped hands, water, like life, is not mine to hold and keep.

I pick Joe up at work, and we follow the directions to our destination, a small town in Connecticut. Arriving three hours later, we meet up with many of the people we have journeyed with from the Wisdom Group weekends. Noticing a few new people, we introduce ourselves as we wait for the teacher to arrive and begin the Friday night opening session of dreaming.

Even though I have experienced dreaming before and have practiced at home with Joe, the anticipation of beginning a formal process, a commitment of ten weekends over one year, makes me edgy. No one knows what to expect, but we talk about our expectations anyway. It is what is done in the face of the unknown. I am not alone in creating illusions of what will be when faced with situations I have no control over.

Saturday morning we are asked to examine how much energy it takes to defend what we know against what we feel. While dreaming I see myself adjusting numerous rear and side view mirrors that surround my body. The vision is a metaphor for the way I manipulate how I react to people to get the best possible reflection of myself returned from them. The revelation helps me recognize how much time I might be spending trying to control a situation in order to preserve an image I have of myself. I know what I want reflected back to me, so that I can continue to define myself. But is that image really me?

The teacher tells us that she loves us on Sunday morning. "I love you," she repeats in her soft, caressing voice as she moves around while we sit dreaming together in a large carpeted room filled with nothing but chairs. "I love you," then adds, "now send and receive this message to yourself." The words stick in my throat even though I'm not attempting to say them out loud. I love you — me — Karyn? I hit resistance, big time. Why does saying that feel so unnatural, disturbing and untrue? I sit with the resistance and the unsavory feeling like a good dreamer and wait for what bubbles up.

I am not disappointed. When I am feeling cut off and separated from the people I am with, I see that I usually accept each person —

warts and all, except myself. No wonder I suffer, believing that I am unworthy sometimes. Look at what I am doing! I generate feelings of isolation because of the way I feel about myself. The habit of not accepting myself is a feedback loop that only I can break. I hear an accented voice that sounds like Don Miguel say, "Silly girl, why do you do that?" I hope when I feel undeserving and left out next time, I remember that it is only me being unloving to me.

In the struggles we choose for ourselves

JOE CAN'T GET THE WAITRESS TO COME TO OUR TABLE SOON ENOUGH; WE SWITCH our seats to the airport bar. I toss back a vodka and grapefruit; the buzz is clean and quick. I order a rare second drink; I'm on vacation, after all, and slip deeper into a euphoria brought on by the vodka and high expectations for my thirteen-day European power journey. I slip off my leather jacket and relish the coolness of the air-conditioning on my back, only slightly self-conscious in my black cotton camisole shirt. I catch the cook checking me out from the bar service window. I like what is reflected back to me; I feel young, pretty and tingly.

That was yesterday. This evening, twenty hours later, I am at Dunderry Park in Ireland, shivering in the cool evening breeze as we sit in a circle outside the main building of the Holistic Healing Center where we are staying for the next few days.

The power journey leader asks us to state our intent. Our intent for this journey or in general? I'm not sure; her words are carried away with the breeze, and I'm not paying attention. Until now, that is, since I will have to have something come out of my mouth in a moment or two. I try to listen to each person, while I allow another part of my mind to do a quick inventory of what my intent may be for whatever it is that I am doing here. I hit upon something and check it for validity. The statement is true, but I feel awkward saying something like this out loud. It sounds arrogant to me, as if I think too highly of myself. Will I declare my intent out loud? I have to decide quickly. I am next.

170

The leader looks at me.

I take a deep breath, look her in the eye and say, "My intent is to be as large as I am destined to be." There — I said it out loud.

I know everyone else is thinking about his or her own admissions, but I am still self-conscious about using the word *large* and *I* in the same sentence.

We are given a dream assignment before we break for bedtime. We are told to ask ourselves to reveal in our dream a belief that limits or causes us unhappiness. After turning out the lights I lie in my twin bed in a charming bedroom for four and find myself defending my intent to myself. I argue its validity from my point of view against the imagined prosecutor in my mind. I catch myself and see how stupid and futile this exercise is. I glean a quick view of myself carrying on this same type of defend/prosecute scenario repeatedly in my life regardless of the issue. A spell of inaction and limitation; a complete waste of time and energy,

I realize I have a choice. I can continue with my internal courtroom drama, hoping for a favorable verdict from the judge I carry within me, or I can look back and replay the scene, speaking my intent aloud, and decide the moment was perfect. I tell myself my statement was perfect, just the way it was and is. I make a cozy nest in the too soft, yielding mattress and fall asleep.

I wake up a few hours later and worry about getting back to sleep. The wheels in my mind start turning. I think of how tired I will be if I don't get back to sleep. How miserable I will feel in the morning and later in the day during the all night Mitote ceremony. The litany of imagined tortures goes on for about five minutes and I yell, "ENOUGH." Let me lie here and be, let me be here resting now and let tomorrow take care of itself.

I lie motionless in my cozy nest and listen to my breathing. A few minutes later a net of warm pin lights knitted into a mystical blanket is lowered onto my body. I fall asleep blissfully. I wake twice more and am able to recreate for myself the same peaceful blanket of bliss that holds me until my consciousness is swallowed by the dark opening of the unknown.

After a holistic breakfast and a short bus ride we split into two groups, one group of men and another larger group of women. Sitting on one of the many hillocks that make up the Hill of Tara in Ireland, our teacher recites a prayer about the Divine Feminine.

I listen with half an ear. I have heard similar words before; while they are beautiful, they don't resonate with me as much as other prayers and teachings have.

She asks the women to share their feelings in this sacred space.

I have nothing to say as I listen to the women speak their words of femininity and goddess-ness.

The day is overcast, and there is no protection from the wind. There are very few trees on Tara, and the view is a wide-open vista of rolling hills. Tara is the site where the Warlord Kings of Ireland were crowned for centuries. There are no monuments or castle ruins, not even a surviving chapel, only the earth on which we sit. It is the earth from which we draw our inspiration and insight into our feminine nature.

Some women speak of body issues and the self-rejection that arises from believing their body is not what it should be. They speak of having been denied their feminine nature in response to past self-rejection because of the erroneous view that femininity and power are mutually exclusive.

I listen respectfully, but their words are blown away with the wind. They speak softly, gently, lovingly and some tearfully. I feel myself distancing from the women. The words do not describe my feminine essence. I feel more Scarlet O'Hara than Divine Womb Mother at times. Not that I don't love my womb. I loved being pregnant and did experience that amazing healing session through my womb. But that is not where I associate my femininity. Everyone has spoken, and I'm ready to stretch and rejoin the men. My name is called. I'm not sure I heard right, as I have not indicated I wanted to share this time. I pause to make sure someone else doesn't answer the call. I resist the urge to stand but project clearly and loudly. I want the women gathered to hear my words.

"I am a Dream Warrior. I am here to tell stories, myths and histories. I am here to tell the story the way I want to hear them. I hear them with a message of freedom — freedom from all tyranny. We tell stories; that is what we do here. So I will tell stories. Stories without apology for being a woman . . . " I pause for a moment realizing alienation and self doubt is not limited to women only " . . . or for being a man. I am a woman and a warrior, and I embrace that."

Back to Dublin before we head west, Joe and I find Dublin Castle within walking distance of our hotel. Old and new buildings surround the castle; it is easy to miss unless you are looking. There are cars parked in the cobblestone courtyard, and business people walk in and out of various doors. We follow signs for tour information and enter a hastily constructed box office.

A young man, who looks to be about nineteen, sits at a government-issue metal desk. He explains that the castle is in use right now. The European Union leaders are meeting at the castle until July. Instead of a tour of the staterooms, there will be a video, a viewing of the excavated tower with its Viking foundation, and a tour of the chapel attached to the castle. We decide to take the tour and wait in a room with a projection screen and long benches sparsely filled with tourists.

The video begins with a history of the castle. Built eight hundred years ago it has never been taken over. The site started as a Viking stronghold and evolved into an English outpost. The castle was built to protect English subjects within its walls from the Irish chieftains who ruled outside the castle moat. The narrator of the video lists various infamous English Chancellors and describes the handover of the castle to the Irish in the last century. The narration finishes at the present time when the castle was chosen to house the E.U. leadership before the European Union elections.

The walls around me have withstood centuries of war, domination, oppression and religious persecution to survive and offer shelter to a new democracy. The E.U. is the beginning of cooperation among nations that killed each other for millennia. Hope, I feel hope, sitting here, crying on a tourist bench with my water bottle and camera.

I enjoy the rest of the Dublin Castle tour but a larger part of me is miserable. The beautiful calm of Dunderry has lifted from my soul. Nobody else wanted to tour the castle, and we didn't hook up with anyone else last night, either. In fact, we ditched a few people, and now I am conflicted about doing so.

I find myself comparing who may be having a better time, the other people in our group or me. I wonder what they are doing, if they are together, laughing and joking, enjoying the city as a tightly knit gang — like we were in Dunderry. I feel abandoned; we aren't going to the Harry Potter movie premier with most of the group. This was supposed to be an unplanned day, but the tour leader purchased fourteen movie tickets. Some people made the list to get a ticket, Joe and I didn't; we didn't know about the list. I don't care about the movie; it is the idea of a list that is eating at me.

Grouchy with Joe by mid-afternoon, I don't want to be alone with him when there are so many interesting people traveling with us. The weather turned cold and Joe is dressed like a tourist for a tropical island instead of rainy Ireland. He needs to change and I could use my leather jacket and an umbrella, and so we are back at our hotel.

It doesn't help my mood to run into the movie ticket holders in the lobby of our hotel. Now I sit in my room with my woeful, childish thoughts. I don't talk about my feelings with Joe, and I don't try to talk myself out of feeling forlorn. I don't want to make them wrong so I can justify the way I feel. I just need to respect the way I feel. And end an old story. But I need action to do that.

Instead of talking myself out of feeling my old wounds — I'm by myself, abandoned by the group, blah, blah, blah — I need to figure out what will make me happy and then create that situation. To make myself happy I need to get out of this hotel room and hook up with some people. I make Joe get up. He has stretched out on the bed, and I'm afraid he will be asleep soon. I tell him I want to go to Trinity College, another tourist spot that's free and within walking distance. I know most of the gang has left for the movies. I don't expect there is much chance of meeting anyone, but we bump into Clare on the street right away, and I invite her to go with us.

My point of view shifts, and I start enjoying myself again. We find our way to the college with the help of a cordial Dubliner. Once on college grounds, we follow signs for the Book of Kells, but by the time we find the right building the museum is closed for the day. We call Clare's roommate to see if she would like to join us for dinner; I don't want to inadvertently ditch anyone else on this trip. She does. We back track to the hotel to pick her up. I notice Joe tries to rush us as we are ordering dinner, and I flash him a deadly look. I let my irritation with my husband go and listen to my dining companion's spiritual adventures while I eat very bad Irish stew.

Later that night, taking a bath in the narrow, deep European tub, I reconstruct the day. I see how projecting my old fears of abandonment altered my perception of some very simple events. Old wounds, potent poison for the soul. Talk about ruining a good time. I am in Dublin, visiting remarkable places, and I felt wretched most of the day. I'm glad my misery surfaced, sort of, because I see so clearly how suffering works. But I don't want to experience those feelings again. It's no surprise when I talk myself out of feeling dejected or go shopping when that uncomfortable emotional acid creeps in and takes hold. Sometimes I indulge in something tasty to eat or an extra glass of wine to avoid feeling an old ache. I probably attack Joe, too, to deflect the pain. Marriage can be a minefield — with all these hidden bombs just below the surface.

I set my intent to remember a dream that will help clarify the day and my desolation. I want to know why I was so relentless in my inability to focus on what I was doing and enjoying the moment before I bumped into Clare. I don't remember the beginning but near the end of the dream I'm given a party favor bag. In the bag under tissue paper are Jennifer's fertilized eggs! "Oh dear," I say, "I didn't think these were still good." Someone replies, "Oh, yeah, they are good, but you need to plant them in a womb soon." I don't know exactly what to do with the eggs and regret that I hadn't taken better care of them. I wake up thinking what the heck am I doing with Jennifer's eggs? I met Jennifer for the first time on this trip. She told me yesterday morning that she was on this trip because she felt stuck in her life. She feels unable to take action, even on the things she wants to do.

The eggs represent the seeds planted in me to create a book to tell the story of my spiritual quest. They appear as Jennifer's in my dream because she is stuck in her life, unable to take action. The eggs symbolize an activity I have not been nurturing for six months. Perhaps if I were doing what I wanted, what stirred my soul, I wouldn't need to compare my life with others so often. And hopefully I would be much less likely to be looking for other people's discontent to match my own.

After checking into our B&B in Kinvarra the following morning, we are back on the bus to visit an Irish farm that is the home of an ancient Dolman. The countryside is rugged and harsh. Rocks coat the pastures, and the gentle rolling grass fields are gone. The cows and sheep must pick their way carefully among the stones to find something to eat. Jim, our bus driver, informs us the farmer may charge an entrance fee because the constant stream of visitors is a disruption to his livelihood. He doesn't charge today, and Jim parks the bus on the narrow road outside the farmer's front gate.

Even from the road, the Dolman is huge. The slabs of rock have to be at least ten by twenty feet long and a foot thick. There are three solid rocks, two long slabs upright, lying parallel to each other lengthwise and another slab lying flat on top. The simplicity and sheer size and weight give the Dolman a solemn, sacred and austere presence. We are quiet and respectful as we circle closer to get a better view from as many angles as we can. People are buried here, according to the plaque declaring the six thousand year old Dolman a National Monument.

Our teacher moves us away from the other visitors and settles us next to a rocky ravine. We are instructed to dream here. I don't hear anything more specific, and the harsh beauty of the landscape forces me to keep my eyes open. The field we are sitting in looks as though the stone used to be all one rock until something split it apart. The seams are filled with wild flowers and grasses that have forced their way up through the hard earth. Tiny blossoms peek out at me from between the stony fissures.

I can only imagine the bleakness of life for the people who lived here six thousand years ago. No modern comforts like heat or hot water, only barren land with a damp cloudy climate. What possessed them to come here? What possessed them to drag these huge stones and create an edifice here atop a hill overlooking the faraway coastline?

I feel the sun on my back and straddle the outcrop of rock as I shift into a more comfortable position. I enjoy the warm stone between my thighs. I feel on top of the world, though I've been at much higher altitudes than I am right now. I look down and see a beautiful wild flower growing between two huge flat rocks. Those people long ago must have been like this flower: tenacious, courageous and undaunted by harsh conditions. The fragile flower looks so beautifully valiant surrounded by the rocks that my heart opens up to its spirit.

Maybe I have it wrong. Maybe the beings; I'm not one-hundred percent convinced that humans built the huge Dolman, thrived on the shear sensuousness of life. There is no middle ground to life up here among the rocks. Life is fought hard for and hard gained. But the ecstasy of surviving and thriving in such an environment would be an achievement that deserves the monument that stands here still. Life feels immediate and sensuous with the sun above and the earth, straddled like a beloved mount, below. I feel as though the two, the sun and the earth, are joined and experience each other through me.

We visit an ancient Cairn next, a dome shaped pile of rocks. Cairns are even older than Dolmans. Maybe the ancients hadn't figured out how to move those big slabs of stones yet, and piling rocks was the most permanent structure they could create. The Cairn has lasted thousands of years.

Will any of our monuments and memorials last as long?

My eyes are drawn to a field of stone next to the cairn. The rocky field is a cemetery, except the headstones are vertical limestone formations that have naturally risen up through the earth. Reminiscent of the movie *Beetlejuice*, I half expect Michael Keaton to pop out and perform a ritual for us.

Our teacher speaks of regrets and how regrets can steal your personal power. She sure knows her stuff; what a perfect place to contemplate one's regrets in life. Better do it now before I end up in a cemetery, dead.

As I step through the surreal limestone headstones, I quickly review my life. I can't say I regret anything I have done. What I regret is the times I was too afraid to experience something. Something new or some emotion I was afraid would overtake me.

I wander a bit until I find a particularly odd looking group of stones. They lean together to form a sharp edged A-frame. I sit down and lower my head. I want to look through the empty A-space the stones created.

The perspective is even eerier closer to the ground. I close my eyes and ask for the wisdom to let go and free myself of the debilitating effect of holding onto, and living with, regret. I also ask to remember without judgment my regret, so that when an opportunity for a new experience comes my way I remember and choose to experience whatever is presented to me. I want to choose the unknown instead of the comfortable. I want to experience the sensuousness of life by embracing the new and let the possibility of regret fall away. The lessons of the Dolman and the Cairn go together so seamlessly that I silently thank the stones, the air, the sun, my companions and my teacher for the opportunity to learn from the very earth herself.

After a day rich with antiquity, wisdom and Irish food, I am lying awake in bed crestfallen. Old wounds and self-loathing are back again. Geez, what is up with that?

I didn't go in for a cup of tea after dinner at the restaurant in the hotel where most of the group is staying. I decided to go for a walk with Joe instead. We ended up farther down the road than we thought. Afterwards, I still didn't go in for a cup of tea. I saw a few people from the group walking outside and didn't want to walk into an almost empty room and feel pathetic, like I missed the boat, like everyone had come and gone, except me. So I went up to our lovely bed and breakfast room across the street with Joe and the nonsense started.

I tell myself I made the wrong decision. Everyone is having fun together tonight but me. I tell myself I crawled up in my room, since I can't relate to anyone, nothing to say and nothing to share. I believe I am too insecure to leave Joe and go by myself.

On and on the stories go, and though I know I am playing an old tape, I can't shake the desolation. At two in the morning I finally get up and go outside to call the kids on my cell phone. Only nine p.m. in New York — they answer, and I tell them that I love them. My mood lifts a bit before going back to bed.

Apparently the abandonment issues are alive and kicking. I have a notion that as bad as I feel now, I will have a chance to dream my experience anew the next day. For now, though, I can only face and feel the loneliness of self-doubt, isolation and abandonment. Self-abandonment really. Nobody has abandoned me; the plight I feel is all in my mind. An interpretation of a situation I repeat in my head out of habit. The absurdity is glaring in its obviousness, but I'm still distraught. Now I know what it means when the teacher warns us to be aware of the things that keep us small. At the Dolman I had the world between my legs. Eight hours later I am quite small with my doubts and self-abusive thoughts.

We are here
to abet creation
and to
witness it

AFTER WAKING UP SOAKING WET FROM A VICIOUS EARLY MORNING HOT FLASH, I pop into the shower. Jim and another couple join us for our first breakfast in an Irish B&B. The freshly cooked food and hot coffee is a treat for my mouth, and I am aware that I have been given a new day to experience the time in whatever way I choose. An Irish breakfast is a delicious way to start. I don't know what it is about Irish sausage, but they are plumper and tastier than the hard little links back home.

Before getting on the bus, we gather behind the hotel across the street. A massive garden filled stone heart sits in the backyard. The teacher speaks of a new day, a chance to live the day with new awareness. It's amazing the way she says out loud what was on my mind only minutes ago. She tells the group it's an extraordinary day, because we are alive and aware. She goes on to say the day is also special, because it is my birthday! I delight in everyone knowing it's my birthday; an event similar to being a bride at her wedding — everybody knows who you are and that the day belongs to you.

We board the bus and head toward the coast. Our destination becomes larger from the bus windows as we wind our way along the coastline. Croagh Patrick, Ireland's Holy Mountain, is in sight. Clouds cover most of the mountain's peak. The view from my bus window brings back memories of Haleakala, a cavernous extinct volcano whose slopes Joe and I rode bicycles down years ago.

179

There is something about a peak of earth being higher than a cloud that makes me want to climb; but we have only ascended a short way when we gather in a narrow valley on the right side of the mountain's path. A seven-foot rock and a stream sit in the middle of the ravine. A small waterfall where rock meets earth creates a natural lyrical backdrop to our teacher's words. Plush grassy slopes filled with wild flowers and bramble bushes hide us from hiking tourists. The elements of our abundant earthly space provide a gorgeous setting as we individually go into a silence of our own making.

I lean left against the cool solid rock. In sensuous contrast, I have the sun warming the back of my neck and right side of my body. I drink in the sound of the little waterfall at my feet, while a breeze lightly lifts the hair from my face. I breathe in the sweet fragrance of the wild flowers and close my eyes to enjoy the gift of my other senses. I hear words fill my heart and mind, and I repeat them to myself so I won't forget. I know the words are not mine but have been given to me in answer to the question of my own existence.

"I am the awareness that allows the sun to be aware of the earth. I am the awareness that allows the air to kiss the water and merge into one. I am the awareness that is God being aware of God."

Leaving the Holy Mountain, we board the bus and make our way to another sacred Irish site. When the bus can no longer negotiate the winding narrow dirt road, we climb our way like goats through hilly pastureland for miles, treading the well-worn path to Carrowkeel Star. Gloria, our friend from our France trip, leads us to a circle of ancient Cairns. Rain threatens as I read a weather worn wooden sign that advertises WWW.CARROWKEEL.COM. I laugh at the contrast between the twenty-first century sign and the surrounding sheep, rocks and sparse meadow; a view I could have witnessed a thousand years ago.

Reaching the nearest and largest Cairn I look through the stone archway. Two candles illuminate the rock igloo interior. No one is inside. A few minutes later we are instructed to visit the closest two Cairns and come back to this one. The closest cairn represents the Father, the next represents the Mother, and the cairn we begin and end at is Unity.

The rain has begun, but my body is as light as a feather as I skip from rock to rock to visit Father Cairn. We are told to only take a moment at each opening and return quickly due to the possibility of a thunderstorm. I breathe in deeply the ancient musty air of the first cairn and exhale my gratitude for being here, for being happy, filled and contented on my birthday. I hop over to Mother Cairn and take an extra moment to peer into her dark womb. This one is not lit with candles and the opening is shrouded in mystery. I breathe deeply again, delighted by the smell of earth and rock mixed with the rain-dampened air.

I turn from the mysterious rock pile and make my way, stone by stone, to Unity Cairn. I jump around and pass the few people who are in front of me. For some unknown reason I want to be there before anyone else. I reach the cairn first, but don't see any of the teachers nearby, so I check under the arch again. I'm startled when I see all three sitting silently inside, looking like modern sentinels of the stones. They signal me to come inside. I twist into a modified limbo to avoid hitting my head on the beam of solid rock that supports the opening of the Cairn. I slither into the damp, opened earth and look for a place to sit. I'm told there is another opening further behind that can fit a few small people and to please sit there.

"Okey-dokey," I reply with feigned fearlessness and crawl carefully into the small dark crevice behind my teachers. Scott is next to join me in my rocky tomb, but when Joe attempts to climb in I tell him he is too big. I'm scared enough being under tons of ancient rocks in the dark without being squished as well. The space is free only for a moment. Then Clare asks to climb in, so that everyone else in the group can squeeze into the Cairn too. I ask her not to block the little bit of light. I don't want to freak out completely.

She tries not to sit on me — while backing into our womb within a womb. We are tightly packed against the stone walls and each other. Kim is the last in and stands outside our crevice. Now when we peer out the narrow opening we look out between Kim's bare brown limbs. Our teacher speaks of life, death and re birth. The womb allusion is complete, as I wait to be birthed and expelled out between Kim's legs.

I want to share the words that came to me on the mountain this morning. I wait until all the teachers have spoken, then ask to share with the group. The teacher tells me to come out and stand in front of her. I tell her I can speak from where I am. I feel self-conscious and would rather remain an anonymous voice in the dark. She insists, and I am birthed out into the small cave. Standing with my teacher's arms supporting me, I say the words I have repeated so often that I already know them by heart.

"I am the awareness that allows the sun to be aware of the earth. I am the awareness that allows the air to kiss the water and merge into one." I take a deep breath before the last verse. I feel the truth of the words but to say them out loud makes me think I sound boastful and blasphemous. I exhale out those thoughts and say what I know to be true.

"I am the awareness that is God being aware of God."

The limits of tyrants

Joe and I have broken off from our traveling companions to sightsee in London for a few days. Westminster Abbey is our first destination. We wander while waiting for our abbey tour guide to arrive on the hour. The first alcove we discover has a stained glass mural with a blond woman holding a cross topped staff. She has a sunlit halo around her head and stands on a red dragon. Kneeling before her is a Bishop with his hat next to his feet. There is an angel near the clergyman holding a replica of the abbey in its outstretched hands. The angel is offering the golden-haired woman the abbey. Unusual for a religious mural. Who is this blond woman, and why is the church bowing at her feet?

The tour begins, and I forget to ask the guide. There are so many other stories here. Over three thousand people are buried in Westminster Abbey. Not in a cemetery outside but buried under the abbey floor and in the giant stone tombs that we explore with our guide and fellow tourists. I'm taken aback by how many generals and war heroes are honored and buried in the Abbey; a place of worship with an ongoing service only forty feet away.

When we stop at the first ever Tomb of the Unknown Soldier at the end of the tour we silently read the inscription. I try to remember if I have ever visited a U.S. place of worship with a war memorial inside. I can't recall any; a physical manifestation of separation of church and state, I presume. Looking around, I can only guess what they really worshiped here centuries ago. Apparently God doesn't build an English empire alone, as the Unknown Soldier monument gives testament to.

Back to a cathedral on our second day in London. Since France, Joe and I are hooked on visiting ancient sanctuaries and abbeys. Seems to be where the action was. Places of worship are what survived the centuries, and the stories they tell are magnificent.

We don't purchase a tour at St. Paul's, deciding instead to explore its grand chapels on our own. My favorite discovery is a doorway with an angel on either side. The angels look nonchalant as they gaze outward from the opening they appear to be guarding. Above the door is an inscription that reads:

THROUGH THE GATE OF DEATH
WE PASS TO OUR JOYFUL RESURRECTION

What a benevolent way to view death — a joyful resurrection, a resurrection for all of us. The doorway says *we* right there in stone. Not only Jesus Christ — *we*. I don't remember hearing about any joyful resurrection waiting for me when I die. Judgment day is the message I heard growing up. We are judged worthy enough to get into heaven or sinful enough to be sent to hell. Nothing about hell here, and appraising the way the angels are looking the other way, I'd say anybody could pass through this doorway.

A new
manifestation
is at hand

PULLED AWAKE AT THREE IN THE MORNING, I AM GREETED BY THE ORANGE-PINK glow of pre-dawn in the eastern window of our English countryside B&B. We have rejoined our companions from Ireland on Magdalene Street in Glastonbury. I enter the bathroom, happy to use the bidet again. What a great invention! This is definitely on my list of what to have in my next, post-kids house. While washing my hands, I catch a glimpse of the moon sliding from behind thinly stretched clouds in the mirror above the sink. I turn around to see where the reflection is coming from and look up through the skylight that is the only window in the room. All I witness is the pink of daybreak. The mirror is the sole perspective available to me; the moon is only visible as an illuminated reflection.

Adoring the moon wrapped in the light of dawn, day merges into night and time does not exist for a moment. I open the windows to let in the cool morning air. The birds chatter as I eat my bowl of fruit and sip the fresh squeezed orange juice the owner of the bed and breakfast left for us late last night. She made up the breakfast tray, though she knew we were leaving at five this morning. The sweet fruit, the romantic four-poster bed, the moon and birds, all of these, make the morning's sunrise a dream come true.

Our tour guides have arranged a private visit, and we are the first group of visitors at Stonehenge today. The monolithic stones are postcard perfect as we approach the site on foot with the park officials. The placements of ancient slabs are a gargantuan Feng Shui arrangement. Whoever or whatever placed these stones was focusing their intent. I gaze up at the colossal, impassive rock circle. What that intent was is a mystery to me.

Gloria leads us single file around the middle of the circle of stones, so that our bodies create an eternity symbol. A voice commands us to stop, and I find myself at the axis of the eternity knot in the center of Stonehenge. Stonehenge and eternity are too immense for me to take in. I ponder the meaning of both and wait to be released from the heart of the circle of stones arranged thousands of years ago.

Set loose, we are free to explore the site on our own for a few minutes. I lay back on a stone that had fallen from the top ring to land askew on the ground. The warm rock beneath my back has no whispered answers for me. The guard reminds us that we are not allowed to lean or sit on the rocks, and I immediately sit up. I mean no disrespect, I say silently to the stone sentry. I wish the slab could speak; tell me its story. The silence is not broken. The mysterious stone isn't talking, not to me anyway.

Our next stop is Avebury, a parade of smaller stones. Each stone has a personality or a rough likeness to an animal. One is an elephant and another a camel. The place feels light and airy; whimsical compared to Stonehenge. Stonehenge loomed heavy, a focus of ancient Druid intent. In contrast, Avebury is a celebration creation. The entire site is spread out over a round plateau surrounded by a trench and encircled by a bumpy embankment. The small humps in the embankment resemble a giant serpent encircling the carefully placed stones.

We gather under a grove of trees that J.R.R. Tolkien is rumored to have visited. The massive tree trunks could have been his inspiration for Treebeard and the Ents. We sit on the rough entangled roots under a canopy of leaves and birds. Eileen takes out a wand she purchased in Glastonbury, and we pass the magical talking stick, and each person is given an opportunity to say goodbye. This is our last day together.

Pat, the oldest member of our group shares a message invigorated with new meaning at Stonehenge. *Sinless, Fearless, Whole, Rejoicing, Now and through eternity!*

The stones do talk! A woman who came all the way from Hong Kong recites a beautiful Buddhist prayer, after our Dublin dinner companion conveys her farewell words in her native French. The beauty of their words and the lyrical lilt of their voices hold us in an international web of intimacy.

I'm not sure what to say; maybe I should share something from London, the angels at St Paul's or the stained glass at Westminster Abbey. The wand is passed to me, and I stand to face my fellow adventurers. I start to say thank you and am cut off with, "Karyn, you are a messenger; you are not small."

Caught being inauthentic, I stamp my foot. Not that I am *not* grateful to everyone here, but that isn't what I want to say. "All right," I begin, as if the words need to be pulled out of my mouth. "The most powerful incident that ever happened to me took place in my living room almost a year ago. I do not doubt what I am or the truth of our teacher's words. So as beautiful as this place is and as wonderful as the last eleven days have been," I pause and look at the seekers gathered at my feet, "you don't need it. Be grateful, silent, open and *feel*. The rest will happen. That is the way truth is." Our closing ceremony under the trees ends, but our individual journeys will not.

Our teacher reminds us that what we have created here, we take with us. "What Karyn said is true," she confirms. "You don't need this setting for anything to happen. It's in you."

June 2004

Forgiveness. We are asked to forgive ourselves for all the self-abuse and unloving things we have heaped upon ourselves. All the silent, cutting, backstabbing little criticisms we utter to ourselves throughout the day. Forgive yourself for not accepting yourself just the way you are, right now, this moment. Forgiveness, now that we are aware of what we are capable of doing to ourselves. Aware of what we *are* doing to ourselves. Forgiveness for yourself, forgiveness given by you to you.

"Forgive me," I whisper to myself. "Forgive me, I didn't know better at the time. Forgive me." A warm flush of tenderness permeates my being as I hear myself answer, "Of course, I forgive you. I love you." Mmmmm, that feels good, I want to sit with this. So I sit in silence with my fellow dreamers, content with the moment.

I lift out of the warm accepting space I am in and read the writing on the walls of my mind. The act of forgiving me, sincerely forgiving myself in my heart, means there is no going back. Forgiving sincerely means I am aware of what I do to myself. Aware of the obstacles I place in my way.

Awareness and forgiveness means I cannot go back and blame myself for being self-abusive. I am aware. And forgiven. There is no more going back to believing my self-sabotage. There are no more excuses for not creating what I want. This scares me. I've no one to blame, not even myself! Awareness. Forgiveness. Powerful acts. I exhale slowly and wonder if I'm ready to let go of my last excuse — me.

July 2004

Newsday printed the Unanimous Declaration of the Thirteen United States of America, otherwise known as the Declaration of Independence in a special fold out section of the newspaper. On July 2, 1776, twelve of the thirteen states passed a resolution of independence. Seeing the declaration in the newspaper is a time saver for me. I have been meaning to bring it up on the Internet. I want to hang the words on a wall in my meditation room at home:

> *"We hold these truths to be self evident, that all men are created equal, they are endowed by their creator with certain inalienable rights, that among them are life, liberty and the pursuit of happiness."*

Even though I want to get the words exactly right, I consider changing men to something more gender neutral — or maybe not. The words are an extraordinary expression of an ideal regardless of when it was written. Life, liberty and the pursuit of happiness is a radical sentiment for an official government document. Endowed with inalienable rights by their creator. Not God, mind you, the document says creator. They knew back then what an explosive concept God is.

I take a moment with my morning coffee and reminisce on the first time I went to a Great Books discussion group. Our first reading was the Declaration of Independence. I never thought much about my country's founding document before that. Stating that life, liberty and the pursuit of happiness belongs to the individual, not God and country, is progressive, even by today's standards. Dig deep into patriotic and conservative religious ideals, and this statement is on the opposite end of the spectrum.

I appreciate the genius and careful selection of words. Reading the rest of the paper I am aware we are still trying to live up to our founding document in this country. I hope the country I love fulfills its promise well enough that the rest of the world will want to adopt the essence of our evolutionary intentions.

There is another string of words already displayed in my special room. I found a faded blue plaque when visiting my sister-in-law's new summer cottage in a town not far from the house where Joe and I go for dreaming weekends. The dusty relic had been left by the previous owners and my sister-in-law told me to keep it when I picked it up out of a box of junk. The inscription is attributable to a fictional character in Richard Bach's novel *Jonathan Livingston Seagull* but the words are Hall Bartlett's, the director, producer and screenwriter of the movie with the same name.

It is good to be a seeker but sooner or later you have to be a finder and then it is well to give what you have found to the world for whoever will accept it.

Some would say it wasn't a coincidence that I found the plaque when I did. Maybe. Mostly I'm grateful for the push the quote gives me towards the laptop when I'm trying to decide whether to write or tackle a domestic chore waiting to be done.

Richard Bach's book was popular when my religious roots were being formed. That is the theme for my third summer service — religious roots that grew wings. I had to look back to see what had brought me here. What was going on when I formed my religious beliefs? What beliefs did I let go; which did I keep? Surprisingly it is the stories of my childhood and the music of my teenage years that helped form my religious perspective. Dr. Seuss, Mary Poppins and the Wizard of Oz all played a part. Bob Dylan, the Vietnam War and the sixties had a hand in it too. Adrienne Rich's *Transcendental Etude* reminds us that we are not given the chance to practice life, but instead "*we take on everything at once before we've even begun to read or mark time, we're forced to begin in the midst of the hardest movement, the one already sounding as we are born."*

I ask my fellow worshipers to share the stories and times that have shaped their religious beliefs. We realize how entrenched our beliefs are in the times we lived.

Going through some old folders in my home office later that month, I find a file called *Dreams etc.* filled with the dreams I wrote down during therapy. Aliens, rummage sale sneakers, and parasites reveal that many dreams are open to interpretation, except for this one in particular. I can still remember seeing the bare walls as I walk through an empty, light filled apartment, happy to finally have my own place. There are sliding glass doors that allow sunlight to pour into the eating area. I turn around to inspect my new kitchen and notice a closet door opposite the sliding glass doors. I walk over to the door, turn the knob and pull the door open.

Inside is a little girl, between seven and nine years old. She covers her face and crouches down low into the farthest corner of the closet. I wonder why she is frightened and hiding then hear gunfire in the distance and realize there is a war going on outside, a guerilla war a block away. My happiness evaporates, and I chastise myself for moving into a war zone. Other people, possibly reporters, come into the kitchen and question the girl. She is coaxed out of the closet, and we see what a beautiful child she is. She explains that the guerilla leader is looking for her and will do anything to find her.

My childhood home was the battleground of my parents. What was comforting and safe by day could transform into a chaotic emotional minefield at night. The defenses I learned dealing with battling self-abusive adults didn't go away when I got older. They follow and stay with me, no matter where or how I try to hide.

* * *

Someone is coming towards the room. I know I will have to get up in a moment to gather with the rest of the Dreamers upstairs. I don't want to go. I want to stay curled up on my aero bed and drift back to sleep. The opening Mitote ceremony a few hours ago was wonderful. "Why screw up a good thing with sleep deprivation and prayers," I mutter to myself as Clare touches my shoulder to make sure I'm awake. I get up despite my resistance and look for my blue shawl. I hear Joe fumbling around in the dark next to the top of the bed when I reach over him to get my water bottle.

"What are you doing?" I say through clenched teeth, annoyed by his scurrying noise.

"I want to put more air in the bed" he replies, while futilely feeling for the power cord that will cause the motor to pump more air into our slightly deflated air mattress.

"I don't want to hear that now!" I spit out. The thought of loud noise in the dead of night sets my nerves on edge. What a stupid idea, what an idiot, I think about my husband as I grab my shawl and shuffle towards the bathroom before I go upstairs. I have to wait in line even at this hour.

By the time I get upstairs the room is almost filled, as it was three hours ago. This time I don't see any unoccupied backjacks. Dreamers, assistants and the teacher surround the altar. The presence of some people at the altar angers me. My foul mood slips further down the scale of emotions. Vibrating at a lower octave, I find a comfortable chair against the wall where I can see but am far enough away from the others so I don't contaminate them with my ornery, contemptuous presence.

Sandy pops up to my left, gives me a kiss hello, and I feel better — for a moment. Why does who sits at the altar make me so angry? I wonder. Why do I care? This isn't nursery school where sitting next to the teacher is an honor — or is it? Do you need a certain aura or level of spirituality to be worthy of sitting at the altar while everyone else is regulated to the outer circles? I don't think so, looking over at those nestled around the six-lighted candles resting on a makeshift altar on the floor. Is it invitation only? Or is it simply whoever has the nerve to sit there like I did earlier tonight?

It was an accident earlier. I saw an open backjack, a maroon one like mine. I didn't want to sit on the floor without back support; you never know how long these ceremonies will go on.

I made a beeline for the backjack and sat my butt down. Then I realized the seat was probably open for a reason. Next to the altar, a teacher or special dreamer (whatever that is) was probably supposed to sit there but hadn't shown up yet. Too bad. They will have to ask me to get up if they need the seat, I thought. I noticed someone point out that I had taken a seat at the altar. The teacher indicated that it was okay, and I relaxed my back into the yielding sturdy canvas. I was too focused in my trance like state from the Circle of Fire song to let any thoughts of not belonging crowd into my almost empty mind. The ceremony that followed transported me into a state of being that left me full of light and love. I floated out when I left the room at midnight.

Why, then, am I so pissed off right now? Why does it matter where anyone sits? Why am I comparing myself to others yet again? I close my eyes and try to listen to the closing ceremony, but it sounds like I have heard it all before. I open my eyes and look around the room. I have been with these people all day. Really. I've had my moment of bliss; so — why do I have to be here now? Why three in the morning? I have to pick up my kids and drive an extra two hours tomorrow. I need sleep. I'm tired. I'm hot.

A voice full of contempt whispers, "You ungrateful bitch." I know the sound of my own voice. I am immediately ashamed, yet at the same time defiant. My only problem at the moment is being unsure of how to tell myself to fuck off. Chastising myself again, for that thought, I try to salvage the moment by tracing my anger and aggravation to its source. But I can't, I won't, I'm hot and tired and relish the near-hate I feel for my present situation.

Words uttered from the altar fade out of my attention when I hear a song hovering in my awareness. "Forgiveness, forgiveness." Recognizing the words and tune from a popular song played numerous times on the radio, I smile. "Even if, even if, you don't love me anymore." I have sung that bit of chorus out loud at home and in the car over the last two months. I always felt the verse had a message other than the obvious one — forgiving an old lover who has moved on. I let the words wash over me and see myself as the lover who has temporarily fallen out of love with me. I am not being loving towards myself right now. I'm being cantankerous, calling myself names and labeling myself ungrateful, because I let some unpleasant feelings bubble to the top. I don't love me right now, that's for sure. But I forgive myself — in this moment some other part of me forgives all. Forgiveness, forgiveness — even if I don't love me anymore.

I am swept up in the sweet loving acceptance I experienced last month when I first sincerely forgave myself for all my self-abusive ways. I forgive me for being unloving and emotionally abusive to myself. It's okay. I'm here. The anger, the annoyance, falls away. My perception shifts immediately. I look around the room again, same faces, same candles, same room. All completely different. All reflecting love. I don't cry. I sit, grateful for the reminder and the ability to forgive.

We receive fragments of holiness, glimpses of eternity

WE LIGHT A FIRE ON THE BEACH AND TOAST MARSHMALLOWS UNDER THE STARS. Garrett asks me if it is true that when we see a star it may already be gone by the time we see it — because the star is millions of light years away. I tell him yes; some of the stars we are looking at right now may no longer exist. We stay by the fire a long time after we are done toasting marshmallows. We can't see this many stars at home, and the night sky is full of them here on Montauk beach, the very end of Long Island. We are hoping to see a shooting star, and we are not disappointed after an hour of stargazing.

Waking up in the middle of the night, I peer up at the night sky through my tent window. I focus on one particularly brilliant pinpoint of light. I am that star shining down at me — only now I am here. Before the light made its way to me, I was a star shining brightly in space. I am receiving my own illuminations. Only the distance of time makes me believe I am one or the other.

Both are different points of perception; time created by distance makes form appear separate. I appear separate from the stars. But I am not. My perception is limited by my human form. My soul is not. My soul is boundless, everywhere and nowhere at once. In infinity, my soul waits for the slow dawning of awareness that is me.

August 2004

The conversation is about faith. We are asked to stop investing our faith in old beliefs about ourselves. Asked to stop investing faith in our current perception of the world around us. We are asked to reinvest our faith in the unknown. We are told that the best place for our faith is in ourselves and in the unknown. A man the teacher is mentoring is assisting this weekend. He told us that he followed Don Miguel to California after the same Omega workshop Joe and I attended in August of 2001. I am uneasy receiving a teaching from someone who started this journey at the same time I did; but I don't need to have faith in this man. Or the teacher. Not even in this process. I have faith in grace. Those moments of grace that have lifted me out of this realm and into something else.

I know as I dismantle my illusions of what it is to be human, I place my faith in moments of awareness, clarity and grace. I can say that I have complete faith in myself. Not my little self that worries about money, my children and the state of the world. I have faith in that other self — the self that is life; the self that loves unconditionally and anonymously; the self that is a pinch of the whole, a reflection of the Divine that is all of us.

I place my faith in the unknown and release the fear when I can. As I open my heart and release the fear, I am filled with Divine presence and knowing. My heart, mind and consciousness collapse into each other to become the awareness that I am. The awareness of life being life. The awareness of Divinity in life. The awareness that is God being aware of God.

Acknowledgments

As with any creation, it takes more than one, and I had all the help in the world. I thank Rita Rivera and Don Miguel Ruiz, two exceptional spiritual teachers and guides, for opening a hidden, mysterious passageway into my heart. They opened the door and ushered me in with love, acceptance and grace. I thank Laura DeSario and Rev. William Feinberg for supporting me while I demonstrated my desire to share my new found faith within our fellowship.

I thank Sylvia Madrigal whose tender loving care and editing brought the book into a presentable, printable form. I also wish to thank Betty Wright and Betsy Lampe of Rainbow Books for encouraging me and walking me through a whole new adventure.

I always knew I was wanted for being exactly what I was — a girl child, a woman to be. That, I have learned, is a great gift in our world, and I thank my mother for the precious gift she gave me. I thank Andrew and Garrett, my children, whose births were the first opening of my heart after a long, conditioned stagnation. I want to thank Joe, my husband, for his openness in accompanying me on this journey, especially when his upbringing told him not to. I thank him for his belief in my abilities, even when I didn't believe in them myself. I thank Kim, my sister, for always being there.

I thank Gloria, my mentor and friend, Gayle and Mystica, my beautiful dreaming companions and all the people who opened their hearts and let me in. Thank you.

With love, happiness and gratitude always,

—Karyn

Connections

www.miguelruiz.com	Don Miguel Ruiz
www.lifemasteryprograms.com	Rita Rivera
www.ligmincha.org	Tenzin Wangyal Rinpoche
www.opencenter.org	New York Open Center
www.eomega.org	Omega Holistic Center
www.UUA.org	Unitarian Universalist Assn.
www.allieroth.com	Allie Roth
www.marshengle.com	Marsh Engle
www.powerfulworkshops.com	Ken Nelson
www.sacredhealingarts.net	Ken Nelson
www.healingtouchCT.com	Amy Okrepkie

Bibliography

Adult Fiction

Millman, Dan. *The Way of the Peaceful Warrior, a Story that Changes Lives.* Novato, CA: New World Library, 1997 Audio Book

Robbins, Tom. *Jitterbug Perfume.* New York: Bantam Books, 1984

Children Fiction

Suess, Dr. *The Sneetches and other Stories.* New York: Random House, 1953

Suess, Dr. *Yertle the Turtle and other Stories.* New York: Random House, 1950

Non-Fiction

Cameron, Julia. *The Artist's Way, A Spiritual Path to Higher Creativity.* New York: Jeremy P. Tarcher/Putnam, 1992

Castaneda, Carlos. *The Active Side of Infinity.* New York: Harper Perennial, 1998

Chopra, Deepak. *How to Know God, The Soul's Journey into the Mystery of Mysteries.* New York: Three Rivers Press, 2000

Clayton, Gayle. *Transformative Meditation.* St. Paul, MN: Llewellyn Worldwide, 2004.

Clements, Alan. *Instinct for Freedom, Finding Liberation Through Living.* Novato, CA: New World Library, 2002

Csikszentmihalyi, Mihaly. *Flow, The Psychology of Optimal Experience, Steps Toward Enhancing the Quality of Life.* New York: Harper Perennial, 1990.

Choquette, Sonia PH.D, *Your Heart's Desire, Instructions for Creating the Life You Really Want.* New York: Three Rivers Press, 1997

Cutler, Howard C. and His Holiness the Dalai Lama. *The Art of Happiness, A Handbook for Living.* New York: Riverhead Books, 1998

Ford, Debbie. *The Dark Side of the Light Chasers, Reclaiming Your Power, Creativity, Brilliance, and Dreams.* New York: Riverhead Books, 1998

Grabhorn, Lynn. *Excuse Me, Your Life is Waiting, The Astonishing Power of Feelings.* Charlottsville, VA: Hampton Roads, 2000

Hawkins, David R., M.D., Ph.D. *Power vs. Force, The Hidden Determinants of Human Behavior.* Carlsbad, CA: Hay House, Inc., 1995

Kornfield, Jack. *A Path with Heart, A Guide through the Perils and Promises of Spiritual Life.* New York: Bantam Books, 1993

Kowalski, Gary. *Science and the Search for God.* New York: Lantern Books, 2003.

Mares, Thuen. *Return of the Warriors, The Toltec Teachings, Vol. 1.* Capetown, South Africa: Lionheart Publishing, 1995

McKenna, Jed. *Spiritual Enlightenment, The Damnedest Thing.* USA: Wisefool Press, 2002

Mindell, Arnold, Ph.D. *Dreaming While Awake, Techniques for 24-hour Lucid Dreaming.* Charlottesville, VA: Hampton Roads, 2000

Myss, Caroline, Ph.D. *Anatomy of the Spirit, The Seven Stages of Power and Healing.* New York: Three Rivers Press, 1996

Ruiz, Don Miguel. *The Four Agreements, A Toltec Wisdom Book.* San Raphael, CA: Amber-Allen Publishing, 1997

Ruiz, Don Miguel. *Beyond Fear, A Toltec Guide to Freedom and Joy.* Recorded by Mary Carroll Nelson. Tulsa: Council Oak Books, 1997

Sluyter, Dean. *The Zen Commandments, Ten Suggestions for a Life of Inner Freedom.* New York: Jeremy Tharcher/Putnam, 2001

Tolle, Eckhart. *The Power of Now, A Guide to Spiritual Enlightenment.* Novato, Ca: New World Library, 1999

Wangyal, Tenzin Rinpoche. *The Tibetan Yogas of Dream and Sleep.* ed. Mark Dahlby. Ithaca, NY: Snow Lion Publications, 1998

Wangyal, Tenzin Rinpoche. *Wonders of the Natural Mind, The Essence of Dzogchen in the Native Bon Tradition of Tibet.* ed. Andrew Lukianowicz. Ithaca, NY: Snow Lion Publications, 2000

Endquotes

1 His Holiness the Dalai Lama and Howard C Culter, *The Art of Happiness — a Handbook for Living* (New York: Riverhead Books, 1998), 32.

2 Normandi Ellis, *Awakening Osiris, The Egyptian Book of the Dead*, (Grand Rapids, MI: Phanes Press, ,1988), 167

3 Unitarian Universalist Association. *Singing the Living Tradition.* (Boston: Beacon Press, 1993), 650

4 Ibid., 657

5 *www.harmonicaconcordance.com/SandyStevenson.htm 11/8/2003*

6 The Unitarian Universalist Association. *Singing the Living Tradition.* (Boston: Beacon Press, 1993), 637

About the Author

Karyn O'Beirne, an MBA graduate with a private consulting practice, has worked in New York Metro area for over twenty years. She enjoys the energy and diversity that NYC offers. Experiential workshops, dinners out and strolling the nooks and crannies of Manhattan are favorite pastimes in the Spring and Fall. Summertime however belongs to the Island and its ocean beaches. After getting the vegetable and herb gardens underway Karyn enjoys the more relaxed pace the season offers.

Karyn is a worship leader and treasurer for the Long Island Area Council for Unitarian Universalist congregations. She often provides Sunday services on the South Shore where she lives with her husband and two sons. Karyn is currently working on her second book which chronicles further explorations into the accessible, divine nature of life.

Karyn O'Beirne invites you to visit her website at
www.Karyn.info